THE CLEAR AND PRESENT TRUTH OF
DANIEL 11

Rapid Movements Publishing

Cover by Pro_Design_Up

Copyright © 2021 by Tory St.Cyr

Printed in the United States of America
All Rights Reserved

Published by Rapid Movements Publishing
Hampton, GA 30228

Other books by Tory St.Cyr may be purchased at www.clearandpresenttruth.com

The author assumes full responsibility for the accuracy of all facts and quotations, as cited in this book.

ISBN: 978-0-578-84076-5

Pictures and illustrations used by permission of creative commons license:

By Diadochen1.png: Captain_BloodDiadochi IT.svg: Luigi Chiesa (talk) This vector image includes elements that have been taken or adapted from this file: Battle icon gladii.svg.derivative work: Homo lupus - Own work; The Macedonian Empire, 336-323 B.C. AND Kingdoms of the Diadochi in 301 BC and 200 BC. Historical Atlas by William R. Shepherd, 1911. Courtesy of the University of Texas Libraries, The University of Texas at Austin., CC BY-SA 3.0, https://commons.wikimedia.org/w/index.php?curid=31138196

By Golan_Heights_relief_v1.jpg: Kbh3rdderivative work: Night w (talk) - Golan_Heights_relief_v1.jpg, CC BY-SA 3.0, https://commons.wikimedia.org/w/index.php?curid=17516799

By Jean-Léon Gérôme - Walters Art Museum: Home page Info about artwork, Public Domain, https://commons.wikimedia.org/w/index.php?curid=18843517

By Thomas Lessman (Contact!) - Own work, CC BY-SA 3.0, https://commons.wikimedia.org/w/index.php?curid=4079843

By Pietro da Cortona - Œuvre appartenant au Musée des Beaux-Arts de Lyon, CC BY-SA 3.0, https://commons.wikimedia.org/w/index.php?curid=32032174

By David Roberts - David Roberts, Public Domain, https://commons.wikimedia.org/w/index.php?curid=10987959

By Hannes Karnoefel - changed wikimedia map, CC BY-SA 3.0, https://commons.wikimedia.org/w/index.php?curid=10495959

By A.Savin (Wikimedia Commons • WikiPhotoSpace) - Own work, FAL, https://commons.wikimedia.org/w/index.php?curid=54520833

By Chamboz at English Wikipedia, CC BY-SA 4.0, https://commons.wikimedia.org/w/index.php?curid=89899000

Other pictures and illustrations were used from a subscription to Freepik.com

This book is dedicated to my older sister, Toya Sobers. Thank you for those Sabbath afternoon discussions on prophecy. You gave me a hunger for the Word of God, which inspired me to write this book.

Contents

Preface	9
WHY DANIEL 11?	11
MEDO-PERSIA	25
GREECE	29
PAGAN ROME	41
PAPAL ROME	61
THE OTTOMAN EMPIRE	73
THE UNITED STATES OF AMERICA	79
TEST YOUR KNOWLEDGE	107
ANSWERS	110
TOPICAL INDEX	110

Preface

Since my teenage years, I have had a steady interest in Bible prophecy—specifically the Book of Daniel. The chapter that always captivated me was Daniel 11, but I found it too difficult to understand. Throughout the years, I have casually read publications and listened to multiple sermons on this chapter. However, many of the publications I have read and sermons I have heard suggested parts of Daniel 11 should be understood as symbolic. Seeing Daniel 11 through a symbolic lens results in Israel becoming a metaphor for the Church, Egypt mutating into Atheism, and the scenes of warfare becoming a symbol for good versus evil.

However, as I began dedicating a significant portion of my time studying Daniel 11, the more impressed I became that this chapter was literal from beginning to end. When Daniel mentioned Egypt, I believe he meant literal Egypt and not a metaphor for religious opposition. When Daniel referred to Israel, I believe he meant literal Israel, not the Church. While I do believe the Church will be persecuted in the last days, I do not believe Daniel 11 is attempting to make that point. Daniel 11 is not about the Church in the last days; it is about the conflict between the nations that encountered God's people.

Since most of this book is based on history, I have added dates and matching historical events to give this book the feel of a timeline. However, I believe the end of Daniel 11 is unfulfilled prophecy, so there are no dates and times towards the end of this book.

The Clear and Present Truth of Daniel 11 will hopefully inspire you to study the Word of God as you have never studied it before. I pray that as you read this book, God will grant you wisdom, knowledge, and an understanding of His Word.

Chapter 1

WHY DANIEL 11?

I believe most authors who have written about Daniel 11 will agree it is a complex chapter. As a matter of fact, I am going to guess that most books written about Daniel 11 begin with a statement declaring this chapter to be among the more difficult chapters to understand.

Why is Daniel 11 so difficult to understand? I have pondered this question for an extended period of time, and I believe what makes Daniel 11 so complex is that this chapter often refers to "he," but we are never told who "he" is. Understand, Daniel 11 is essentially a narration of the prophetic events that involve world powers. However, as the angel revealed these events, Daniel was not given the names of the kings or empires that would one day play a role on prophecy's stage. The angel only described these kings and empires as "he" or "they." This ambiguity is what makes Daniel 11 so difficult to understand. However, I also realize that this ambiguity is necessary to maintain the "prophetic time continuum" (Yes, I love prophecy, and yes, I watch too much Sci-fi). In other words, had Daniel 11 provided the names of the kings and empires, then we would have an apparent dilemma on our hands. Can you imagine if Julius Caesar knew in advance that his senators would kill him? The Roman Senate would've been killed off before knowing who Julius Caesar was! Or what if the Roman Senate foresaw that Julius would become a dictator? The Senate would've likely killed the popular ruler as a baby. If Daniel 11 were written this directly, then kings and empires probably would have destroyed the world prematurely by focusing all their efforts on changing the inevitable. So I praise God for the vagueness of Daniel 11, but I am also confident that the God who made it vague can also make it plain.

In order to simplify this chapter, we first need to decipher the structure of Daniel 11.

The Structure of Daniel 11
Repeat and Expand

Daniel 2,7,8, and 11 all reveal the rise, fall, and careers of the world's greatest empires. While each chapter uses different components and symbols, it should be understood that they each tell the same story. Students of Bible prophecy should know that Daniel 2 is reiterated in Daniel 7, with Daniel 7 providing additional information. Daniel 7 is then restated in Daniel 8, with Daniel 8 providing further insight. Every time Daniel repeats this prophecy, he provides us with more information. The term for this reiteration with additional information is known as "Repeat and Expand." Daniel 11 is also a *repeat and expansion* of this prophecy; however, Daniel 11's repeat and expansion is unique from the prophecies that preceded it. Daniel 2 focuses on an image made of various metals, while Daniel 7 and 8 feature wild beasts. However, Daniel 11 makes no mention of belly and thighs of brass or iron and clay feet. This chapter makes no mention of four-headed leopards or goats with great horns. This notable difference between chapter 11 and chapters 2,7, and 8 suggests that Daniel 11 should carry a literal interpretation.

The literalness of Daniel 11

Some prophecy scholars apply a literal interpretation to Daniel 11 until they reach the end of the chapter. Many of these scholars believe that from verse 40 and onward, Daniel 11 morphs into symbolism. Egypt, which was literal at the beginning of the chapter, becomes Atheism at the end of the chapter. The glorious land, which was Israel at the beginning of the chapter, transforms into the Church at the end of the chapter. The symbols of war and bloodshed that were prevalent throughout the earlier parts of the chapter become metaphors for the spreading of the gospel and the Mark of the Beast. While I don't consider myself a Bible scholar, I agreed with this viewpoint for much of my adult life. It wasn't until I began writing this book that I began to see that by applying a symbolic understanding to the end of Daniel 11, I was breaking one of the most basic rules of prophetic interpretation.

At an early age, I was told that whenever we are dealing with Bible prophecy, we are to interpret the prophecy literally unless there is clear evidence that a symbolic interpretation is necessary. For example, in Revelation 12:1, we see a woman clothed with the sun. Clearly, it's impossible for a human to reach the sun, let alone be clothed with it. The woman is evidently symbolic. In verse 15 of the same chapter, we see a serpent cast water out of its mouth in order to drown this same woman. Is there any question this is symbolic? Of course not. Can you imagine the size a serpent would need to be in order to drown someone with water from its mouth? Clearly, the serpent should not be interpreted literally. This basic rule of prophetic interpretation prevents us from taking symbolic components and applying a literal interpretation to them or taking literal components and applying a symbolic interpretation to them. However, should this rule be discarded when it comes to Daniel 11? Isn't Egypt still a literal country? Why would Egypt be symbolic of anything other than the nation at the northeastern corner of Africa? The region of Palestine is still on the map today. Why then does the glorious land spiritually get repurposed as the Church? Understand, Daniel 11 gives us no reason to apply a symbolic interpretation to the last five verses of this chapter. If Daniel 11:40-45 is made to be symbolic, then what prohibits anyone from making Daniel 11:1-39 symbolic?

This may come as a surprise to many of you, but Daniel 11's focus is not on Israel or the Church. Daniel 11 speaks of kings and princes; it speaks of nations and world powers. You will soon see that minimal attention is given to the persecution of the Jews, half a scripture is dedicated to the Crucifixion of Christ, and the Papal persecution of the Dark Ages is briefly mentioned. Let me be clear: Daniel 11's focus is political, not religious. If you disagree, I challenge you to go through each verse of this chapter and notate how many verses focus on the persecution of Jews or Christians and how many verses focus on the political conflicts between kingdoms and empires. Once you see Daniel 11 for what it really is, you will realize that this chapter is not intended to be symbolic; it's intended to be literal.

Why symbolic?

I've pondered why some of us run from the literalness of Daniel 11 when we get to the end of the chapter. It is my opinion that there are two main reasons behind this. The first reason comes from the fact that the end of Daniel 11 is considered unfulfilled prophecy. This fact reveals the first reason—we are simply uncomfortable with any end-time prophecy that alludes to the Nation of Israel. This, unfortunately, produces a domino effect and forces us to symbolize other components of this chapter that should also be taken literally. Egypt becomes Atheism. Edom, Moab, and Ammon become a unique group of believers, and Israel is forced to be the Church. It is interesting to note that, while everything is believed to become symbolic after verse 40, the King of the North continues to be a literal entity. If everything after verse 40 is symbolic, wouldn't the King of the North also become symbolic?

But I digress. If Egypt is literal at the end of Daniel 11, then the Glorious Land must also be literal. If the Glorious Land is literal, then that small area of the world where Palestine and Israel sit obtains a level of relevancy in Bible prophecy. And if this area of the world obtains relevancy, then we may feel that this would take our focus from the tactics of the Man of Sin and place them on the city of Jerusalem.

While I understand why some would apply symbolism to this part of Daniel 11, we must also be careful not to discard one truth in order to protect another. Two things can be true. I reject the belief that we should focus on the earthly city of Jerusalem, while at the same time, I believe that Jerusalem has a part to play in end-time events. That statement may sound like a contradiction until you realize Evangelicals are focused on Israel from a religious standpoint, but Daniel 11's focus on Israel is from a political standpoint.

The second reason why we focus on a symbolic ending to this chapter is that we aren't quite sure what message Daniel 11 is conveying. When I first began studying Daniel 11, I assumed it was a replica of Revelation 13. Knowing Revelation 13 ends with the Mark of the Beast resulted in me trying to place Daniel 11 in that same bucket. Forcing Daniel 11 to mirror Revelation 13 is like taking a square block and forcing it into a round hole. You must understand, Daniel 11 does not *mirror* Revelation 13, it *parallels* it. Revelation 13 reveals the final conflict from a spiritual perspective; however, Daniel 11 exposes the conflict from a political perspective.

Think about it...Daniel 11 could've easily expounded on Israel's struggles during the reign of Alexander the Great, but instead, it focused on the wars between the divided Greek Empire. It would've been simple for Daniel 11 to detail the intricacies of Christ's Crucifixion and the destruction of Jerusalem, but you will see that both of these events are held to one verse out of a possible 45 verses. Why? The answer is simple: Daniel 11 is not telling the story of the Church; it is telling the story of the State. Once I realized this fact, I stopped trying to force Daniel 11's agenda to fit my own. It was then that I stopped trying to force Emperor Constantine and his Sunday Law into the storyline. At that point, I stopped trying to make the chapter about the persecution of the Christian Church. I decided to allow Daniel 11 to give me an understanding instead of superimposing my understanding into Daniel 11.

Once I allowed Daniel 11 to tell me its story, I realized I must take Daniel 11 at face value. While some components of the prophecy can be a figure of speech, the overall structure of Daniel 11 is literal. How do we interpret a literal prophecy? Simple. If the scripture says Egypt, it means Egypt—not France or Atheism. If the scripture says Israel, this is not the Church nor the United States of America. Israel is Israel. Daniel 11 does not end with the Mark of the Beast, nor the Loud Cry. Daniel 11's focus is precisely what the majority of the chapter describes—the conflict between nations.[1]

The prophetic theme of Daniel 11

A prophetic theme is a recurring detail or underlining characteristic that becomes part of a prophecy's identity. Studying the Book of Daniel, I discovered chapters 2,7,8, and 11 all have prophetic themes. However, if you closely observe these four prophecies, you will see that each prophecy contains one component that is used to introduce the next prophetic theme.

---

[1] While the prophecies of Daniel 11 maintain a literal structure, parts of the chapter may contain metaphorical elements.

In chapter 2, Nebuchadnezzar had a dream. In his dream, four kingdoms were represented by a statue. The golden head represented Babylon, the silver chest and arms symbolized Medo-Persia, the brass belly and thighs were Greece, and the iron legs and feet revealed different phases of Rome. It should be clear that the pervading characteristic of chapter 2 is the metals that formed the statue. These metals are Daniel 2's theme.

Now, please notice what Daniel tells the king before he interprets his dream: "*And wheresoever the children of men dwell, **the beasts of the field** and the **fowls of the heaven** hath he given into thine hand, and hath made thee ruler over them all.*" Daniel 2:38

Interestingly, as Daniel begins revealing the interpretation of Nebuchadnezzar's dream, he makes it known to the king that the beasts of the field and fowls of heaven are in the king's hand. This is not a coincidence.

The next time Daniel receives a vision regarding these four kingdoms, guess how they are symbolized? By *beasts of the field* in which some have wings like the *fowls of heaven*! Notice how Daniel 7 reintroduces these four empires:

> "And four great beasts came up from the sea, diverse one from another." Daniel 7:3

> "The first was like a **lion**, and had **eagle's wings**..." Daniel 7:4

"And behold another **beast**, a second, like to a **bear**..." Daniel 7:5

"After this I beheld, and lo another, like a **leopard**, which had upon the back of it **four wings of a fowl**..." Daniel 7:6

"After this I saw in the night visions, and behold a fourth **beast**..." Daniel 7:7

Do you see this? Daniel 2 declared King Nebuchadnezzar was the ruler over the *Beasts of the field* and the *fowls of heaven*. Remarkably, in Daniel's next vision, these four kingdoms are symbolized as beasts of the field or beasts with wings of a fowl. Little did Daniel know that the statement he made in chapter 2 would become the theme of chapter 7.

However, it does not end there. Notice how Daniel 7 describes the fourth Beast:

"After this I saw in the night visions, and behold a fourth beast, dreadful and terrible, and strong exceedingly; and it had great iron teeth: it devoured and brake in pieces, and stamped the residue with the feet of it: and it was diverse from all the beasts that were before it; and **it had ten horns**. I considered the horns, and, behold, there came up among them another **little horn**, before whom there were three of the first horns plucked up by the roots: and, behold, in this horn were eyes like the eyes of man, and a mouth speaking great things." Daniel 7:7-8

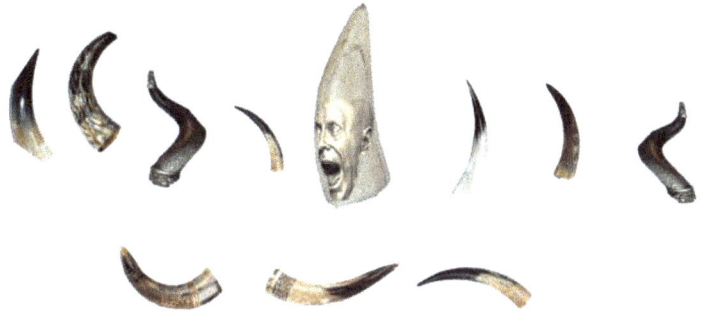

This is interesting! The beasts of the field and fowls of heaven are the symbols of chapter 7, but now another component is introduced. Daniel's description of the fourth beast focuses on horns. The horns mentioned in chapter 7 become the theme of Daniel's next vision! Notice what each beast has in chapter 8:

"Then I lifted up mine eyes, and saw, and, behold, there stood before the river a ram which **had two horns**: and the two horns were high; but one was higher than the other, and the higher came up last." Daniel 8:3

"And as I was considering, behold, an he goat came from the west on the face of the whole earth, and touched not the ground: and the goat had a **notable horn between his eyes**." Daniel 8:5

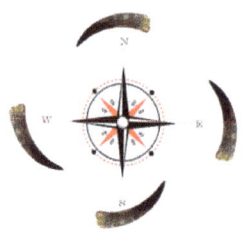
"Therefore the he goat waxed very great: and when he was strong, the great horn was broken; and for it came up **four notable ones** [horns] toward the four winds of heaven." Daniel 8:8

"And out of one of them came forth a **little horn**, which waxed exceeding great, toward the south, and toward the east, and toward the pleasant land." Daniel 8:9

This is amazing! Daniel 7 introduced us to the horns on the fourth beast, and now all the beasts of Daniel 8 have horns! A component of one vision declared the theme of the next vision. This same pattern continues in Daniel 8. Can you find the component of chapter 8 that determines the theme of chapter 11? The answer is found in Daniel 8:4,5,8, and 9. Notice the common element in each of these scriptures:

> "I saw the ram pushing **westward, and northward, and southward**..." Daniel 8:4
>
> "And as I was considering, behold, an he goat came from the **west** on the face of the whole earth..." Daniel 8:5
>
> "...the great horn was broken; and for it came up four notable ones toward the **four winds** of heaven..." Daniel 8:8
>
> "And out of one of them came forth a little horn, which waxed exceeding great, **toward the south, and toward the east**..." Daniel 8:9

Daniel 8 introduces these world powers with a new component: Each empire is now identified by the compass direction from which it originated or the compass direction of its conquests. Please note that these compass points become the theme of Daniel 11!

Daniel 11's theme is interwoven into the main characters of the chapter. These two characters are called the King of the North and the King of the South! We can see how the directional component of Daniel 8 now becomes the theme of Daniel 11. It is important to understand that just as Daniel 7 stayed with the beast theme and Daniel 8 remained with the horn theme, Daniel 11 stays with the cardinal direction theme.

The segments of Daniel 11

Considering the vision of Daniel 11 occurs after the fall of Babylon, this vision begins with the kings of Persia, transitions to Greece, and ends with Rome. We know which nations are highlighted in Daniel 11, but we don't know how the chapter is partitioned for these nations. Which scriptures refer to Persia? How do we determine when the chapter transitions to Greece? Lastly, how do we determine when Rome steps into the spotlight?

The good news is that we don't have to guess how Daniel 11 is partitioned. In His wisdom, God placed built-in indicators into this chapter to let us know when a transition occurs. You may have read these indicators but didn't realize they were signals. The rule for these indicators is simple: The way a kingdom rises is the same way that kingdom falls. Notice how Daniel 11 has these transitions already built-in:

Persia is introduced:

"And now will I shew thee the truth. Behold, there shall **stand up** yet three kings in Persia..." Daniel 11:2

Persia ends, and Greece begins:

"And a mighty king shall **stand up**, that shall rule with great dominion, and **do according to his will**." Daniel 11:3

Greece ends, and Rome begins:

"But he that cometh against him **shall do according to his own will**, and none shall stand before him: and **he shall stand in the glorious land**, which by his hand shall be consumed." Daniel 11:16

Rome ends:

"**And he shall plant the tabernacles of his palace between the seas in the glorious holy mountain**; yet he shall come to his end, and none shall help him." Daniel 11:45

We don't have to guess when Daniel 11 transitions from one kingdom to the next. God has already done the work for us; all we need to do is apply it.

As we begin to understand the structure of Daniel 11, we will start to see that God is giving us a glimpse into the roles that the world's empires will serve right before the end of the world. This is *Why Daniel 11* is so important. If we can determine who "he" is and who "they" are, we may be able to see just how close we are to the Second Coming of Christ.

Chapter 2

MEDO-PERSIA

Kingdom Profile

Media-Persia was an ancient Empire, based in Western Asia, founded by Cyrus the Great.

- **Period of dominance**: 539 BC - 331 BC
- **Popular ruler(s)**: Cyrus the Great
- **Modern location**: Iran
- **Notable activity**: Commanded the restoration and build-up of Jerusalem in 457 BC.
- **Location in Daniel 11**: Verses 1-2

Daniel 11:1 - Also I in the first year of Darius the Mede, even I, stood to confirm and to strengthen him.

At the end of the previous chapter, Gabriel said to Daniel, *But I will shew thee that which is noted in the scripture of truth.*[2] The phrase—"*that which is noted*" in the original language is *râsham*, which means it was inscribed or committed to writing. In essence, the angel is telling Daniel that the events he will be shown have already been inscribed as the truth. They are already recorded in the heavenly ledgers, and nothing can prevent them from occurring. Daniel 11 is simply a detailed account of these events that would take place in the future. The angel begins this prophetic narration by telling Daniel that in the first year of Darius the Mede's reign, he visited the king to confirm and strengthen him.

522 - 486 BC

- Persia provokes Greece -

Daniel 11:2 - And now will I shew thee the truth. Behold, there shall stand up yet three kings in Persia; and the fourth shall be far richer than they all: and by his strength through his riches he shall stir up all against the realm of Grecia.

Initially, the Medes were co-conquerors with the Persians, but Daniel revealed that this would soon change: In Daniel 7, the bear *raised itself on one side*, and in Daniel 8, one of the ram's horns was *higher than the other*. Both the bear and the ram represent the Medo-Persian Empire. However, the bear's higher side and the ram's higher horn both foreshadowed that the Persians would one day subdue the Medes, making Persia the world's undisputed superpower. Daniel 11 refers to the empire after Persia became dominant.

---

[2] Daniel 10:21

The three Persian kings that ruled after Cyrus the Great were Cambyses II, Bardiya (sometimes called Gaumata), and Darius I. The fourth king was Xerxes I, who was also known as Ahasuerus in the book of Esther. In the original language, this verse can be interpreted that Xerxes would *stir up* the whole world against Greece. However, some interpret this verse to mean that the whole realm of Greece (Athenians, Spartans…etc.) was stirred up to stop Persia. Both interpretations are historically accurate as both empires were stirred up. History says that after 480 BC, the Persian Empire entered a period of decline after Xerxes attempted to invade Greece but failed.[3]

As the Persian Empire declined, another power was rapidly gaining momentum. The world was moving toward a showdown between the current world power and a new world power.

---

[3] Persian Empire, HISTORY, A&E Television Networks, October 8, 2019, https://www.history.com/topics/ancient-middle-east/persian-empire

Chapter 3

GREECE

Kingdom Profile

Greece was a Hellenistic civilization from the western Mediterranean region of the world whose culture, philosophy, science, and art still impact modern societies.

- **Period of dominance**: 331 BC - 168 BC
- **Popular ruler(s)**: Alexander the Great
- **Modern location**: Greece
- **Notable activity**: Original King of the North and King of the South.
- **Location in Daniel 11**: Verses 3-16

- The rise of Alexander the Great -

Daniel 11:3 - And a mighty king shall stand up, that shall rule with great dominion, and do according to his will.

`336 BC`

Alexander the Great

The stirring up of the Grecian Empire culminated in the rise of a mighty king. This mighty king was Alexander the Great. He rose to power and used Xerxes' failed invasion of Greece as a pretext to attack Persia.

In 333 BC, Alexander the Great defeated the last Persian king of the Achaemenid dynasty—Darius III. This marked the end of the Persian Empire and the beginning of Alexander's reign as the undisputed leader of the known world.

- Greece splits -

Daniel 11:4 - And when he shall stand up, his kingdom shall be broken, and shall be divided toward the four winds of heaven; and not to his posterity, nor according to his dominion which he ruled: for his kingdom shall be plucked up, even for others beside those.

`323 BC`

Alexander the Great now stood as the undisputed leader of the known world; however, his supremacy was short-lived. After subduing the Persian Empire, he contracted a mysterious illness and died in 323 BC.[4]

- Diadochi Wars -

`322-281 BC`

Alexander's sudden death created a power struggle among his generals, top officials, relatives, and friends. These warring factions, also known as the

---

[4] How Alexander the Great Conquered the Persian Empire, History, October 31, 2020, https://www.history.com/news/alexander-the-great-defeat-persian-empire

Diadochi, divided the territories and plunged the empire into a civil war known as the Diadochi Wars. Alexander the Great had a child, but he was killed by one of the Diadochi; therefore, Alexander's lineage or *posterity* never inherited the kingdom. Even though there were multiple warring factions, four of the Diadochi ultimately emerged as rulers of the newly divided Greek Empire.

- Lysimachus - ruled Thrace and much of Asia Minor.
- Cassander - ruled Macedonia and Greece.
- Ptolemy I Soter - ruled Egypt, Palestine, Cilicia, Petra, and Cyprus.
- Seleucus I Nicator - ruled the remainder of Asia.

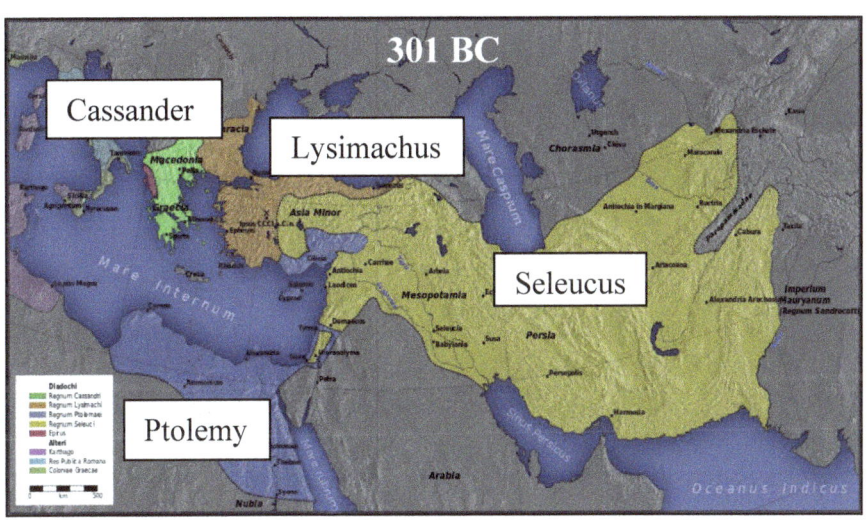

A map of the divided Greek Empire and the Diadochi that ruled its territories.

Just as prophecy foretold, Alexander's kingdom was divided among the four winds of heaven. Before the end of the Diadochi wars, Lysimachus would become King of the North, Seleucus would become King of the East, Ptolemy would become King of the

South, and Cassander would become King of the West. The four divisions of Greece are consistent with Daniel's previous visions:

"After this I beheld, and lo another, like a leopard, which had upon the back of it four wings of a fowl; **the beast had also four heads**; and dominion was given to it." Daniel 7:6

"Therefore the he goat waxed very great: and when he was strong, the great horn was broken; and for it came up **four notable ones toward the four winds of heaven**." Daniel 8:8

Daniel 11:5 - And the king of the south shall be strong, and one of his princes; and he shall be strong above him, and have dominion; his dominion shall be a great dominion.

As ruler of the south, Ptolemy became a great king; however, prophecy foresaw that Seleucus would become even greater.

Before becoming King of the East, Seleucus was a Babylonian governor, but he was forced to flee from Babylon During the Diadochi wars. Seleucus retreated to Egypt and served as one of Ptolemy's generals. However, in 312 BC, Seleucus, with Ptolemy's help, took Babylon and much of the east, which made Seleucus the King of the East.[5]

In 281 BC, Seleucus's army met Lysimachus's army at the Battle of Corupedium. Seleucus defeated

---

[5] Wasson, Donald L. "Seleucus I Nicator." Ancient History Encyclopedia. Last modified May 29, 2012. https://www.ancient.eu/Seleucos_I/.

Lysimachus, which made him ruler of the northern territory in addition to the east.

Seleucus, who once fled Babylon and served as a general under Ptolemy, would not only become stronger than Ptolemy, but *his dominion shall be a great dominion.*

- Seleucids of the north vs. Ptolemys of the south -

Daniel 11:6 - And in the end of years they shall join themselves together; for the king's daughter of the south shall come to the king of the north to make an agreement: but she shall not retain the power of the arm; neither shall he stand, nor his arm: but she shall be given up, and they that brought her, and he that begat her, and he that strengthened her in these times.

255 BC

By the third century BC, the empire consisted of two main divisions—the north, ruled by Antiochus II, and the south, ruled by Ptolemy II. Eventually, conflicts erupted between these two kings, which led to the establishment of a peace treaty. To honor this agreement, Antiochus II divorced his wife Laodice and married Ptolemy's daughter Berenice. However, after Ptolemy's death, Berenice lost the favor of her husband. In essence, she was not able to *retain the power of the arm.*

In 246 BC, Antiochus brought his ex-wife, Laodice, back to his court, which proved to be a fatal mistake. Soon after reuniting with Laodice, Antiochus was poisoned, and Berenice was murdered along with her infant son.[6]

---

[6] Bromiley, International Standard Bible Encyclopedia: A-D p.144

- The Third Syrian War -

246-241 BC

Daniel 11:7 - But out of a branch of her roots shall one stand up in his estate, which shall come with an army, and shall enter into the fortress of the king of the north, and shall deal against them, and shall prevail:

After Ptolemy II's death, Berenice's brother, Ptolemy III, became the King of the South. Prophecy also called him *a branch of her* (Berenice's) *roots*. After Ptolemy learned of his sister's death, he raised an army to avenge her. In 246 BC, Ptolemy waged a war campaign against Laodice's newly crowned son, Seleucus II. Ptolemy's war campaign succeeded, and in exchange for peace, Seleucus awarded Ptolemy with new territories along the northern coast of Syria.[7]

Daniel 11:8 - And shall also carry captives into Egypt their gods, with their princes, and with their precious vessels of silver and of gold; and he shall continue more years than the king of the north.

245 BC

During the invasion of the north, Ptolemy III also recovered the sacred idols that were previously taken by the Persians. In addition to those idols, silver and gold were also confiscated and brought back to Egypt.[8] Though Ptolemy reigned longer than Seleucus II, Ptolemy never again invaded Seleucid territory.

244 BC

Daniel 11:9 - So the king of the south shall come into his kingdom, and shall return into his own land.

Now that a portion of Seleucid lands was in

---

[7] "Syrian Wars," Encyclopædia Britannica, November 01, 2020, https://www.britannica.com/topic/Syrian-Wars
[8] Jerome, Commentary on Daniel 11.7-9

Ptolemy's possession, the King of the South returned to Egypt. However, Seleucus II was determined to regain the lost territory. In 244 BC, the northern king took Babylonia, Mesopotamia, and northern Syria.[9] [10]

- The War of the Brothers -

Daniel 11:10 - But his sons shall be stirred up, and shall assemble a multitude of great forces: and one shall certainly come, and overflow, and pass through: then shall he return, and be stirred up, even to his fortress.

239-236 BC

During the conflict between Seleucus II and Ptolemy III, Seleucus's younger brother, Antiochus Hierax took control of Asia Minor. After Seleucus's campaign to regain the territory previously taken by Ptolemy, he turned his attention to the north to recover territory taken by his brother, Hierax. This conflict between the two sons would historically be known as the War of the Brothers.

Seleucus initially defeated Hierax; however, after creating an alliance with nations that were hostile toward the Seleucid Empire, Hierax crushed Seleucus's army at Ancyra (236 BC). After his victory at Ancyra, Hierax realized his alliances provoked a conflict back home with the king of Pergamum.

As the scripture says, Hierax was *stirred up, even to his own fortress*. However, after returning home, the conflict with the king of Pergamum resulted in Hierax's expulsion from Anatolia.[11]

---

[9] "Seleucus II Callinicus," Encyclopædia Britannica, November 02, 2020, https://www.britannica.com/biography/Seleucus-II-Callinicus
[10] Rolf Strootman, "Seleucus," Encyclopædia Iranica, online edition, 2015, available at http://www.iranicaonline.org/articles/seleucid-kings (accessed on 16 April 2015).
[11] "Antiochus Hierax," Encyclopædia Britannica, November 02, 2020, https://www.britannica.com/biography/Antiochus-Hierax

- The Battle of Raphia (The Fourth Syrian War) -

Daniel 11:11 - And the king of the south shall be moved with choler, and shall come forth and fight with him, even with the king of the north: and he shall set forth a great multitude; but the multitude shall be given into his hand.

217 BC

The next major battle between the King of the North and the King of the South occurred in June of 217 BC in the modern Palestinian city of Rafah. This fourth major war featured Antiochus III as the King of the North and Ptolemy IV as the King of the South. This war, also known as the Battle of Raphia, displayed thousands of infantry, cavalry, and several war elephants.

This verse accurately declared that Ptolemy IV would come forth and fight with Antiochus III; however, it also prophesied the outcome of this conflict. History confirms that Antiochus lost the war of Raphia at the hands of Ptolemy.[12] Daniel confirmed the *multitude was given into his hand.*

Daniel 11:12 - And when he hath taken away the multitude, his heart shall be lifted up; and he shall cast down many ten thousands: but he shall not be strengthened by it.

After Ptolemy IV's victory at Rafah, he returned to Egypt to celebrate his triumph. Scripture reveals that Ptolemy was so caught up in his achievement that he missed the opportunity to capitalize off his victory and destroy the Seleucid Empire once and for all. According to history, Antiochus had lost over ten thousand soldiers in the conflict and was vulnerable at the conclusion of this war. However, instead of pursuing Antiochus, Ptolemy elected to go back to Egypt and celebrate. This act allowed Antiochus to regroup and

---

[12] " Syrian Wars," Encyclopædia Britannica, November 02, 2020, https://www.britannica.com/topic/Syrian-Wars

rebuild his army.[13] This is why the scripture says Ptolemy was not *strengthened* by this victory.

200 BC

- The Battle of Panium (The Fifth Syrian War) -

Daniel 11:13 - For the king of the north shall return, and shall set forth a multitude greater than the former, and shall certainly come after certain years with a great army and with much riches.

The Battle of Panium was fought in Golan Heights.

The next major conflict between the north and south took place in the summer of 200 BC. Antiochus III strategically timed this conflict as Ptolemy IV had recently died, and his heir, Ptolemy V, was still a child.

The conflict began after Antiochus invaded and occupied Ptolemaic territories in Asia Minor. After the Ptolemaic commander Scopas re-conquered parts of that province, Antiochus gathered an even larger army than he had at Rafah and confronted the Ptolemaic army. Antiochus would be victorious at the conclusion of this war, completely annihilating the Ptolemaic army.[14]

186 BC

- The Great Egyptian Revolt -

Daniel 11:14 - And in those times there shall many stand up against the king of the south: also the robbers of thy people

---

[13] Uriah Smith, "Daniel and the Revelation" Review and Herald Publishing Association Hagerstown, MD 21740
[14] " Antiochus III the Great," Encyclopædia Britannica, November 03, 2020, https://www.britannica.com/biography/Antiochus-III-the-Great

shall exalt themselves to establish the vision; but they shall fall.

Turmoil that began during the Fifth Syrian war came to a climax. Ptolemy V returned to Egypt only to find his kingdom in full revolt. It is unclear how this revolt began, but the nation's economic troubles and high taxation likely led the emboldened Egyptians to mutiny.

There are differing views on the meaning of "*the robbers of thy people*," but in the original language, it means *the sons of the oppressors*. Some believe the phrase refers to a Jewish sect, and others believe it refers to the Romans; however, I believe it refers to the ancestors of Israel's first oppressors—Egypt. According to history, Egyptian insurgents brought violence and bloodshed to the Ptolemaic Empire. Whole villages and cities were burned to the ground while their citizens were massacred or enslaved. The 20-year revolt finally ended in 186 BC with the defeat of the insurrection's leader Chaonnophris.[15] The Egyptians tried *to stand up against the king of the south*, but they ultimately would fail.

175 BC

- Antiochus Epiphanes and the Revolt of Judas Maccabeus -

Daniel 11:15 - So the king of the north shall come, and cast up a mount, and take the most fenced cities: and the arms of the south shall not withstand, neither his chosen people, neither shall there be any strength to withstand.

In 175 BC, Antiochus IV (also known as Epiphanes) rose to power in the North. In 169 BC, he invaded Egypt and captured the King of the South (Ptolemy VI). The scripture declared that Antiochus

---

[15] Johstono, P. (2016). "7 Insurgency in Ptolemaic Egypt". In Brill's Companion to Insurgency and Terrorism in the Ancient Mediterranean. Leiden, The Netherlands: Brill. https://doi.org/10.1163/9789004284739_008

would *take the most fenced cities*, and history confirms Antiochus's campaign against the south was met with much success as he conquered all of Egypt with the exception of Alexandria.

Antiochus had a strong desire to Hellenize (spread Greek culture) the subjects of his kingdom. However, his efforts to Hellenize the empire brought him into direct conflict with the Jews who, prior to Epiphanes, had a level of independence regarding their religion and culture. The conflict began after Antiochus appointed a new high priest in Jerusalem. Soon afterward, a civil war ensued between the old high priest and the new high priest. Remember, the scripture declared that *neither his chosen people* would withstand. And just as predicted, Antiochus took Jerusalem by storm in 167 BC and enforced its Hellenization. On pain of death, the Jews were forbidden to perform any Jewish rites, including the worship of Yahweh. In their temple, an altar of Zeus was erected, and sacrifices were made to honor false gods.[16] In 164 BC, Judas Maccabeus, the leader of the anti-Greek Jews, led a revolt against the generals of Antiochus and defeated them. In 164 BC, Judas destroyed the altar of Zeus and reconsecrated the Temple.

- A new King of the North -

Daniel 11:16 - But he that cometh against him shall do according to his own will, and none shall stand before him: and he shall stand in the glorious land, which by his hand shall be consumed.

---

[16] "Antiochus IV Epiphanes," Encyclopædia Britannica, November 13, 2019, https://www.britannica.com/biography/Antiochus-IV-Epiphanes

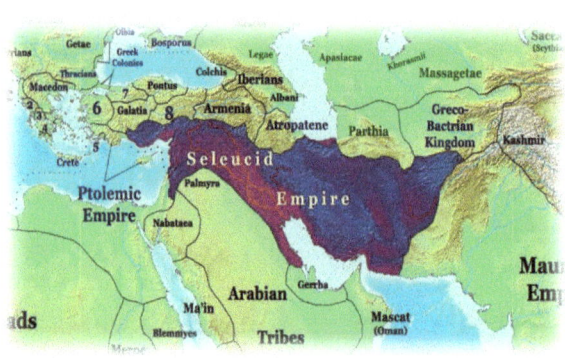

At the height of its power, the Seleucid Empire spanned Anatolia, Persia, the Levant, Mesopotamia, and what are now Kuwait, Afghanistan, and parts of Turkmenistan.

As powerful as this kingdom was, Daniel foreshadowed it would not last when he declared, *he that cometh against him shall do according to his own will.* History confirms the Seleucid Empire fell prey to a power rising from the west. In 64 BC, the northern Empire was annexed to this power as it became the new King of the North.[17] According to Scripture, no other power would be able to *stand before* this rising kingdom—including Jerusalem, which was conquered by the Roman general Pompey in 63 BC. Verse 16 tells us that this rising power would eventually stand in the glorious land and consume it. Whether the world was ready or not, a new world power had arrived on earth's stage.

---

[17] Sicker, Martin (2001). Between Rome and Jerusalem: 300 Years of Roman-Judaean Relations. Greenwood Publishing Group. p. 39. ISBN 978-0-275-97140-3.

Chapter 4

PAGAN ROME

Kingdom Profile
The ancient empire centered on the city of Rome that ruled the known world for five centuries.

- **Period of dominance**: 168 BC - 538 AD
- **Popular ruler(s)**: Julius Caesar, Constantine the Great, Justinian I
- **Modern location**: Europe
- **Notable activity**: Crucifixion of Jesus, Destruction of Jerusalem
- **Location in Daniel 11**: Verses 17-30

- Julius Caesar, Cleopatra VII, and Mark Antony -

Daniel 11:17 - He shall also set his face to enter with the strength of his whole kingdom, and upright ones with him; thus shall he do: and he shall give him the daughter of women, corrupting her: but she shall not stand on his side, neither be for him.

Even though the focal point of Daniel transitions to a new power, we must still decipher who that power is and where we are on its timeline. According to the image of Daniel 2 and the beasts of Daniel 7 and 8, Rome was the world power that succeeded the divided Greek Empire. History confirms that the Seleucid Kingdom was completely absorbed into the Roman Empire, making it the new King of the North.

The next question we need to determine is where does verse 17 place us on Rome's timeline. I believe the phrase *daughter of women* is our biggest clue. While the phrase itself is somewhat obscure, a number of scholars believe it refers to the most notable Egyptian queen, Cleopatra VII. The Cleopatrian lineage originated from a marriage between the Seleucid North and the Ptolemaic South. Cleopatra I was the daughter of Antiochus III, who was betrothed to Ptolemy V of Egypt.[18] This lineage of popular Greek women gained much of its notoriety when Cleopatra VII came into contact with a powerful Roman Consul named Julius Caesar. Shortly before Julius became involved with Cleopatra, he fought and won the Gallic Wars. These wars greatly extended Roman territory as prophecy declared he would *set his face to enter with the strength of his whole kingdom*. Not only did Roman supremacy reign in the north, but it also reigned in the south, including Egypt. The *upright ones*

58 BC

---

[18] "Cleopatra I Syra," Encyclopædia Britannica, June 12, 2008, https://www.britannica.com/biography/Cleopatra-I-Syra

may be a reference to Jerusalem, which eventually became a Roman province.

In 49 BC, Julius found himself in the midst of a civil war with another Roman Consul named Pompey Magnus. Julius' pursuits led him to Egypt, where he became romantically involved with the *daughter of women*—Cleopatra VII. Cleopatra's father placed her and her brother under the guardianship of the Roman Empire. It was in this manner that Cleopatra was given to the King of the North and as a result, Julius appointed her as the queen of Egypt. Cleopatra would later have her brother, Ptolemy XIV, poisoned confirming the Scripture which declared that her reign would be full of *corruption*. Though she had a passionate affair with Caesar, her loyalties remained with Egypt, which is why verse 17 says, she shall not *be for him*.

Caesar Giving Cleopatra the Throne of Egypt

- Conspiracy against Julius Caesar -

Daniel 11:18 - After this shall he turn his face unto the isles, and shall take many: but a prince for his own behalf shall cause the reproach offered by him to cease; without his own reproach he shall cause it to turn upon him.

Verse 18 brings our focus back to Julius Caesar. After his victory over Pompey, Caesar turned his attention to the Iberian Peninsula to destroy the remaining opposition forces led by Pompey's two sons. However, the war against Pompey would become the catalyst for Caesar's downfall. The prince is Caesar's close friend; a magistrate named Decimus Brutus. This politician will conspire so the same *reproach* or shame that Julius brought upon Pompey and Rome will be placed back upon Julius Caesar.[19]

44 BC

- The Assassination of Julius Caesar -

Daniel 11:19 - Then he shall turn his face toward the fort of his own land: but he shall stumble and fall, and not be found.

The Death of Caesar

After Julius Caesar crushed his opposition, he turned *his face toward the fort of his own land*—Rome. Julius Caesar returned to Rome, where he was elected dictator for life. On March 15, 44 BC, Caesar arrived at the Senate, where he was assassinated. According to Eutropius, around 60 men participated in the assassination, in which he was stabbed 23 times.[20] Prophecy foretold what would happen once Julius Caesar turned his face toward Rome; he would *stumble* and *fall*.

27 BC

- The reign of Augustus Caesar -

Daniel 11:20 - Then shall stand up in his estate a raiser of taxes in the glory of the kingdom: but within few days he shall be destroyed, neither in anger, nor in battle.

After Julius Caesar's assassination, his great-nephew, Augustus Caesar, became Rome's first emperor. In the original language, the phrase—"*a raiser*

---

[19] Wasson, Donald L. "The Murder of Julius Caesar." Ancient History Encyclopedia. Last modified May 15, 2015. https://www.ancient.eu/article/803/.
[20] Woolf Greg (2006), Et Tu Brute?—The Murder of Caesar and Political Assassination, 199 pages—ISBN 1-86197-741-7

of taxes," literally means "one who causes an oppressor to pass through" or "one who causes an exactor to pass through." The passage thus refers to a king who would send oppressors or exactors throughout the realm. Many commentators have understood this reference to be a tax collector, which was the very embodiment of royal oppression. The Bible confirms that Augustus was known for imposing a great tax upon the whole empire. The Gospel of Luke recorded the following:

> "And it came to pass in those days, that there went out a decree from Caesar Augustus, that all the world should be taxed." Luke 2:1

Some may interpret the *raiser of taxes* phrase as a reference to Augustus making everyone pay more in taxes; however, history seems to indicate that Augustus actually lowered taxes for many due to the census he took of the entire Empire. It appears he made sure everyone paid their fair share, which lowered taxes for many. Regarding this taxation, the Ancient History Encyclopedia states the following:

> "Augustus imposed a regular census – the duty of the censor – to provide a fair assessment of the provincial tax burden, resulting in a fairer collection of tax revenue."[21]

According to Daniel, a few years after this census and taxation, Augustus would die. The official records of Augustus reveal that he made at least three general surveys of the Roman Empire (28 BC, 8 BC, and 14 AD[22]).

---

[21] Wasson, Donald L. "Reforms of Augustus." Ancient History Encyclopedia. Last modified May 25, 2016. https://www.ancient.eu/article/905/.
[22] Res Gestae Divi Augusti i. 8

History confirms Augustus died in 14 AD, *within a few days* of his last census. The emperor did not die in *anger* or *battle*; Augustus died at an old age of natural causes.[23]

- The reign of Tiberius Caesar -

Daniel 11:21 - And in his estate shall stand up a vile person, to whom they shall not give the honour of the kingdom: but he shall come in peaceably, and obtain the kingdom by flatteries.

The meaning of vile in the original language is "one who is lightly esteemed, despised, or lowly regarded." Tiberius was known as a dark, reclusive ruler who was called "the gloomiest of men."[24] Tiberius was considered to be an emperor who ascended to the throne *peaceably* due to the fact most men in his position ascended through war, conquest, or the assassination of the previous leader.

Tiberius *obtained* the throne through his mother's maneuvering, who married Augustus and had Tiberius adopted as his son.[25]

31-70 AD

- The Crucifixion of Christ and destruction of Jerusalem -

Daniel 11:22 - And with the arm overflown from before him, and shall be broken; yea, also the prince of the covenant.

"Arms" is a reference to the military power of Rome. The event described

The Siege and Destruction of Jerusalem

---

[23] Wasson, Donald L. "Reforms of Augustus." Ancient History Encyclopedia. Last modified May 25, 2016. https://www.ancient.eu/article/905/.
[24] Pliny the Elder, Natural Histories XXVIII.5.23; Capes, p. 71
[25] Wasson, Donald L. "Tiberius." Ancient History Encyclopedia. Last modified July 19, 2012. https://www.ancient.eu/Tiberius/.

by Daniel is the siege and desolation of Jerusalem that occurred in 70 AD. Just as a flood overflows the walls of a dam, the walls of the Holy City would eventually be *overflown* by the Roman army. Daniel 9:26 refers to this same flood when it says, "*the prince that shall come shall destroy the city and the sanctuary; and the end thereof shall be with a flood.*"

In Daniel 11:22, the *Prince of the Covenant* refers to the One Daniel prophesied would *confirm the covenant with many.*[26] This Prince that Daniel refers to can only be Jesus Christ of Nazareth. In 31 AD, Jesus was arrested by the Jewish leaders and crucified by the Roman soldiers.

430 AD

- The rise of a new King in the South -

Daniel 11:23 - And after the league made with him he shall work deceitfully: for he shall come up, and shall become strong with a small people.

Remember, the underlying theme of Daniel 11 is the King of the North vs. the King of the South. However, from the time Egypt became a Roman province, Rome stood as the King of North *and* the King of the South. So, staying true to its north vs. south theme, verse 23 skips over 400 years of Roman supremacy and brings us to the point when the next King of the South would rise.

In the fifth century, Rome faced a serious threat

---

[26] Daniel 9:27 KJV

at its northern border. Large numbers of Barbarian tribes began invading the empire. While some of these tribes were small and insignificant, a number of them played a major role in Bible prophecy by causing the downfall of the Western Roman Empire. Daniel 11:23 highlights the fact that one of these tribes momentarily became the King of the South.

Early in the fifth century, a Barbarian tribe known as the Vandals crossed into Roman territory and eventually sailed to North Africa. In 430 AD, the Vandal king Genseric conquered the North African city of Hippo Regius.[27] This conquest resulted in a treaty between the Vandals and the Romans, which gave the Vandals ownership of North African territory.

However, Daniel informed us that *after the league made with him, he shall work deceitfully.* History confirms Genseric chose to break that treaty in 439 AD when he seized the African city of Carthage.

The Vandals began as a small insignificant sect of people, but they became a powerful rival of the Roman Empire under King Genseric. Prophecy was correct; he became *strong with a small people.*

- The Vandals conquer Carthage -

Daniel 11:24 - He shall enter peaceably even upon the fattest places of the province; and he shall do that which his fathers have not done, nor his fathers' fathers; he shall scatter among them the prey, and spoil, and riches: yea, and he shall forecast his devices against the strong holds, even for a time.

After the capture of Carthage, Genseric and the

---

[27] "The Vandal conquest," Encyclopaedia Britannica, accessed on November 14, 2020, https://www.britannica.com/place/North-Africa/The-Vandal-conquest

Vandals held essential territory within the Roman Empire.[28] Carthage was known as one of the most prosperous regions

The territory held by the Vandals solidifying them as the King of the South.

within the Roman Empire and was a major supplier of grain to the city of Rome. This is consistent with Bible prophecy that says, "*He shall enter peaceably.*" In the original language, the word for peaceably is "shalvah." Shalvah can also be translated as "prosperity." Considering verse 24 mentions "fattest places" and "riches" and "spoil," the context seems to suggest that prosperity is the focus of this verse. Therefore, the proper rendering of this text should be "*He shall enter into prosperity—even the fattest* (most fertile) *places of the* (Roman) *province.*" At that time, the "fattest" place was clearly North Africa. King Genseric took North Africa's wealth by taking the property of its citizens and distributing it amongst the Vandals.

455 AD

Also, in 455 AD, Genseric and the Vandals sacked the city of Rome. However, they did not destroy the city; they

The sacking of Rome

---

[28] "The Vandal conquest," Encyclopaedia Britannica, accessed on November 14, 2020, https://www.britannica.com/place/North-Africa/The-Vandal-conquest

simply stripped it of its wealth. According to history, the Vandals looted great amounts of treasure from the city while damaging objects of cultural significance.[29] The looting, raiding, and destruction left by the Vandals was so significant that even today, the destruction of property is called an act of vandalism. Yes, the word Vandalism is derived from the Vandals of North Africa.

> "The looting, raiding, and destruction left by the Vandals was so significant, that even today the destruction of property is called an act of vandalism."

Genseric also strategized (*forecast his devices*) to stay one step ahead of the Romans. In 457 AD, Majorian, the Eastern (Byzantine) Roman emperor, began assembling a fleet which he intended to use against the Vandals. However, Genseric was informed of the impending attack and in 461 AD, executed a preemptive strike destroying the Roman vessels before they were ready for action.

With territory, wealth, and military might, the Vandals became the official King of the South.

468 AD

- Battle of Cape Bon -

Daniel 11:25 - And he shall stir up his power and his courage against the king of the south with a great army; and the king of the south shall be stirred up to battle with a very great and mighty army; but he shall not stand: for they shall forecast devices against him.

Hostilities continued to escalate between the Vandals and the Romans. The Vandals continued

---

[29] Peter Heather, The Fall of the Roman Empire: A New History of Rome and the Barbarians, p. 378.

raiding, pillaging, and looting the coastline of the Mediterranean, which made them a threat to the future existence of the Roman Empire—A threat that *stirred up the power* and determination of Rome against *the King of the South*.

In 468 AD, the Eastern and Western Roman Empires combined forces and invaded the King of the South. The massive expedition into Vandal territory consisted of 1,113 ships and over 50,000 military personnel.[30][31] This *very great and mighty army* was one of the most extensive military operations in Roman history! Unfortunately for Rome, this large expedition ended in failure. According to history, the Romans anchored their whole fleet at Cape Bon instead of moving directly against Carthage. Genseric asked and was granted a five-day truce in order to negotiate a peace treaty. However, during the truce, Genseric attacked the Roman fleet, which caught them off guard. The surprise attack destroyed over 600 Roman vessels and thousands of military personnel.[32] The scriptures foretold that *he shall not stand*, which was evident when the Roman navy limped back home.

According to Daniel, the Vandals were successful because of the *devices they forecasted against* the Romans. In essence, the strategy Genseric employed against the Romans was the source of the Vandal's success against the Roman Empire. But what was his strategy?

---

[30] Priscus, fragment 42; translated by Colin D. Gordon, The Age of Attila: Fifth Century Byzantium and the Barbarians (Ann Arbor: University of Michigan, 1966), p. 120f. See Gordon's note 11 on the emendation.
[31] Heather, P. (2006). The Fall of the Roman Empire: A New History (1st ed.). New York City: Oxford University Press
[32] Mark, Joshua J. "Gaiseric." Ancient History Encyclopedia. Ancient History Encyclopedia, 13 Dec 2014. Web. 05 Dec 2020.

- The war strategy of King Genseric -

Daniel 11:26 - Yea, they that feed of the portion of his meat shall destroy him, and his army shall overflow: and many shall fall down slain.

King Genseric's success against the Roman Empire was simple but impactful. History records King Genseric used Roman ships against Rome. When Genseric took Carthage in a surprise coup, it immediately gave him access to the Roman fleet docked at the Carthage harbor.[33] Not only did Genseric take control of the Roman fleet, but many of the captured captains switched allegiances. The former Roman fleet was now a Vandal fleet; this is why Daniel declared *they that feed of the portion of his* [Rome] *meat shall destroy him* [Rome]. The fleet taken from Rome added to the existing Vandal fleet enabling King Genseric to rule the Mediterranean Sea.

`530 AD`

- Vandal kings struggle for the throne -

Daniel 11:27 - And both these kings' hearts shall be to do mischief, and they shall speak lies at one table; but it shall not prosper: for yet the end shall be at the time appointed.

Often this verse is given an ambiguous interpretation. Most commentators generalize these two kings as representing a time when alliances were broken and coalitions violated. However, when we look at other verses in this chapter, we see that each verse in Daniel 11 must relate to a specific event in history. Therefore, verse 27 must also refer to a specific event that can be verified by the historical record.

In 530 AD, a conflict arose with the Vandalic Empire. Hilderic, the grandson of Genseric, was the king

---

[33] Vandals, Romans and Berbers: New Perspectives on Late Antique North Africa. United Kingdom: Taylor & Francis, 2017.

of the Vandals. Hilderic had a cousin named Gelimer who was in line to succeed him. However, according to Gelimer, Hilderic was going to change the laws of succession so that the kingship stayed within Hilderic's family.[34] Thus, Gelimer plotted behind Hilderic's back to take the throne from his cousin. In 530 AD, Gelimer killed his cousin and became the king of the Vandals. Now we see that the two kings who sat at the same table telling lies were Hilderic and Gelimer. Unfortunately for them, neither king's plans would prosper. Soon after Gelimer killed Hilderic, Rome invaded the Vandalic Empire and Gelimer died in Roman captivity.

533 AD

- Justinian the Great -

Daniel 11:28 - Then shall he return into his land with great riches; and his heart shall be against the holy covenant; and he shall do exploits, and return to his own land.

Emperor Justinian I rose to power as the emperor of the Byzantine (Eastern Roman) Empire in 527 AD. At the time of his ascension, the government's treasury was well-funded and possibly had a surplus of gold. Justinian soon exhausted the treasury of the government by misappropriation and overspending the Empire's money. As a result, Justinian turned his attention to his subjects and over-taxed them. Regarding this taxation by the Byzantine Emperor, Procopius, a 6th-century historian, states the following:

> "No sooner had he thus disposed of the public wealth than he turned his eyes towards his subjects, and he straightway

---

[34] Merrills, A.H. "The Secret of My Succession: Dynasty and Crisis in Vandal North Africa." Early Medieval Europe 18.2 (2010): 135–159. Web.

robbed great numbers of them of their estates, which he seized with high-handed and unjustified violence, haling to court, for crimes that never happened, men both in Byzantium and in every other city who were reputed to be in prosperous circumstances."[35]

According to Daniel, Justinian's taxation on Byzantium and other cities was how the Byzantine Emperor *returned great riches back to his land.*

...and his heart shall be against the holy covenant...
Daniel also revealed that Justinian's *heart shall be against the holy covenant*. The question is—What is meant by the Holy Covenant? In the Word of God, the Holy Covenant pertained to the promise God made to Israel. The third book of the New Testament says this:

> "To perform the mercy promised to our fathers, and to remember his **holy covenant**." Luke 1:72

We should understand that this Covenant between God and Israel was updated in the New Testament. The updated Covenant says,

> "For this is the covenant that I will make with the house of Israel after those days, saith the Lord; I will put my laws into their mind, and write them in their hearts: and I will be to them a God, and they shall be to me a people." Hebrews 8:10

We must understand that Israel no longer refers to a particular race or ethnicity. Israel pertains to all who

---
[35] Procopius. United Kingdom: W. Heinemann, 1935, p. 231

have given their hearts to Christ. This truth is why Paul made the following declaration to the Galatians:

> "There is neither Jew nor Greek, there is neither bond nor free, there is neither male nor female: for ye are all one in Christ Jesus. And if ye be Christ's, then are ye Abraham's seed, and heirs according to the promise." Galatians 3:28-29

So, the new Covenant pertains to God's Church, which is made of Jews and Gentiles, bond and free, male and female.

In order to understand who or what came up against God's covenant, we need to understand why anyone would be against God's Covenant. The biggest reason why someone would be against God's Covenant is revealed at the end of Hebrews 8:10, which says — *and I will be to them a God, and they shall be to me a people.* So the New Covenant results in Jehovah being their God, and they being the people of Jehovah. The motivation for someone against this covenant is if they want to be God. Have you heard of any supernatural entities that may have a desire to be God? If not, see Isaiah 14:14, which reveals that Satan wants to like the Most High.

Now that we understand Satan has the motive to be against the covenant, we must also be aware that Satan works through governments and religious institutions to achieve his goals. History shows the institution he used was the Christian Church! And he achieved this by deceiving the Church into believing the Bishop of Rome had authority over all the other Bishops of the Church. Eventually, this authority was expanded into the belief that the Bishop of Rome had dominion over all of Christianity. Ellen White[36] makes the following statement regarding this transition from Christ to the Bishop of Rome:

> "To secure worldly gains and honors, the church was led to seek the favor and support of the great men of earth, and having thus rejected Christ, she was induced to yield allegiance to the representative of Satan—the Bishop of Rome.
> It is one of the leading doctrines of Romanism that the pope is the visible head of the universal church of Christ, invested with supreme authority over bishops and pastors in all parts of the world." *Story of Redemption* p. 327

It was during the reign of Justinian that the Bishop of Rome gained supremacy over all the other Bishops. Notice how Uriah Smith points to this historical transition:

> "When Justinian was about to begin the Vandal war in A.D. 533, an enterprise of no small magnitude and difficulty, he wished to secure the influence of the bishop of Rome, who had then attained a position in which his opinion had great weight throughout a large part of Christendom. Justinian therefore took it upon himself to decide the contest which had long existed between the sees of Rome and Constantinople as to which should have the precedence, by giving the preference to Rome in an official letter to the pope, declaring in the fullest and most unequivocal terms that the bishop of that city

---

[36] Seventh Day Adventists view Ellen White's commentary as inspired by God.

should be chief of the whole ecclesiastical body of the empire."[37]

The Roman Empire carried out Satan's plan by enacting decrees that took the Church's attention away from God and placed their hopes in sinful men. This was how Rome, through Justinian, was *against the holy covenant.*

...and he shall do exploits, and return to his own land.
Justinian also wanted to restore the empire to its former Roman glory.[38] This desire was marked by a partial restoration of the territories that had been taken by many of the Barbarian tribes. In essence, Emperor Justinian did *exploits*, to *return* [restore] *his own land.*

`533 AD`

- Vandalic War -

Daniel 11:29 - At the time appointed he shall return, and come toward the south; but it shall not be as the former, or as the latter.

At the time appointed, Rome returned to the south. Africa was the first kingdom on Justinian's re-conquest tour. Of the multiple battles that occurred between the Vandals and Romans, two major offensives are emphasized in the history books. According to the Encyclopaedia Britannica,

"...the King defeated two major efforts of the Romans to overthrow him, that of the

---

[37] Uriah Smith, *Daniel and the Revelation*, Washington, D.C. Review & Herald Pub. Assn., (1907). pp. 275-276
[38] The Middle Ages (eBook). N.p.: Lorenz Educational Press, 1999.

emperor Majorian in 460 and that led by Basiliscus in 468."[39]

The Vandals were almost always successful against Roman invasions, but two of those invasions were significant defeats for the Roman Empire —the Battle of Cartagena in 460 AD and the Battle of Cape Bon in 468 AD. Daniel made sure we understood that this final invasion of 533 AD would *not be as the former* (Cartagena) *or the latter* (Cape Bon) invasions, which ended in Rome's defeat.

533 AD

Daniel 11:30 - For the ships of Chittim shall come against him: therefore he shall be grieved...

In verse 30, we see a transition unfolding. The first half of this verse relates to the end of the Vandalic dispensation; the latter half of this verse relates to another phase of the Roman Empire, which is why the second half of this verse is expounded upon in the next chapter. For now, let us see how the Vandal kingdom ended.

Chittim is a general term for all islanders of the Mediterranean Sea.[40] The "*ships of Chittim*" is most likely a reference to the Vandal fleet, which ruled the Mediterranean for over a century. Before the Vandalic War, the Vandal fleet was diverted to eradicate an internal revolt in Sardinia. It was this diversion that allowed the Roman soldiers to bypass the Vandal fleet and make landfall. The Vandals' strength was its navy, but now they were forced to meet the Romans on land. This resulted in the King of the South being *grieved* by

---

[39] The Editors of Encyclopaedia Britannica, "Gaiseric," Encyclopædia Britannica, https://www.britannica.com/biography/Gaiseric, access date - December 06, 2020
[40] "H3794 - Kittiy - Strong's Hebrew Lexicon (KJV)." Blue Letter Bible. Accessed 8 Dec, 2020. https://www.blueletterbible.org//lang/lexicon/lexicon.cfm?Strongs=H3794&t=KJV

the Roman Empire. Justinian destroyed the Vandals and restored North Africa to Rome.

Chapter 5

PAPAL ROME

Kingdom Profile

The religio-political system known as the Papacy, which rose to supremacy after the fall of the Western Roman Empire and dominated Christianity.

- **Period of dominance**: 538 AD - 1798 AD
- **Popular ruler(s)**: Bishops of Rome
- **Modern location**: Vatican City
- **Notable activity**: Deceived the Christian world into the belief that the Sabbath was changed from the seventh day of the week to the first day of the week. Persecuted the saints.
- **Location in Daniel 11**: Verses 30-36

529-534 AD

- The Code of Justinian -

Daniel 11:30 - ...and return, and have indignation against the holy covenant: so shall he do; he shall even return, and have intelligence with them that forsake the holy covenant.

While Emperor Justinian experienced success in his campaign to *return* Rome's lost territory, his focus became centered upon a collection of Roman laws he compiled known as the Code of Justinian. They were known as civil laws, but because the church was not separate from the state, many of these laws also pertained to church matters—and this is where Rome's *indignation against the holy covenant* began.

Codex Justinianus

In the Code of Justinian, there is a letter from Justinian addressed to Pope John II, which states the following:

> "We hasten to bring to the knowledge of Your Holiness everything relating to the condition of the Church, as We have always had the greatest desire to preserve the unity of your Apostolic See, and the condition of the Holy Churches of God, as they exist at the present time, that they may remain without disturbance or opposition. Therefore, We have exerted Ourselves to unite all the priests of the East and subject them to the See of Your Holiness..." *Thomas William Allies The*

Formation of Christendom, Volume VI, pp 115-116.

Another excerpt from the Code of Justinian states the following:

> "We desire that all peoples subject to Our benign Empire shall live under the same religion that the Divine Peter, the Apostle, gave to the Romans... (1) We order all those who follow this law to assume the name of Catholic Christians, and considering others as demented and insane."[41]

Emperor Justinian's recognition of the Catholic Church and the Roman Bishop's authority was the beginning of what Daniel called the *indignation against the holy covenant*. The reason the authority given to the Bishop of Rome relates to the indignation against the holy covenant should become clear as we remember what the covenant entails.

> "For this is the covenant that I will make with the house of Israel after those days, saith the Lord; I will put my laws into their mind, and write them in their hearts: and I will be to them a God, and they shall be to me a people." Hebrews 8:10

Notice the New Covenant language declares God will place His law in the minds of His people and write those laws in their hearts. The scripture continues by informing us that Jehovah would be their God, and they would be God's people. However, Daniel 7 warns us that

---

[41] Immanuel Kant, The Philosophy of Law (The Lawbook Exchange, Ltd., 2001), 9

Papal Rome would emerge in an attempt to change the laws of the Covenant, and God's people would be given into the hands of this power. Notice how the Book of Daniel reveals this:

> "And he shall speak great words against the most High, and shall wear out the saints of the most High, and **think to change times and laws: and they shall be given into his hand** until a time and times and the dividing of time." Daniel 7:25

The "he" in Daniel 7 is the Papacy. This is the same organization that the Code of Justinian empowered by giving supremacy to its head—the Bishop of Rome. The Papacy would later seek to speak great words against God and think to change God's times and laws (Sabbath). Through decrees, Emperor Justinian placed the church into the hands of the Roman Bishop, where it would remain for 1,260 years.

Now do you understand why the Code of Justinian was the beginning of the indignation against the holy covenant? If the "head of the church" thought to change the law that is supposed to be in the hearts and minds of God's people and the people accept the change...then they are under the Papacy's covenant, not God's. And if the people are under the Papacy's covenant, how can they be God's people?

Justinian studied religion and gained an understanding of the Catholic faith, or as Daniel says, he shall *have intelligence with them that forsake the holy covenant.*

538 AD

- Papal supremacy -

Daniel 11:31 - And arms shall stand on his part, and they shall pollute the sanctuary of strength, and shall take away the daily sacrifice, and they shall place the abomination that maketh desolate.

Taking a closer look at Daniel 11:31, we can see a parallel to the second half of Revelation 13:2, which says, "...*and the dragon gave him his power, and his seat, and great authority.*"

What John the Revelator calls "*Power*," Daniel the Prophet calls "*Arms*." Both words describe the true source of the Empire's power—its armies.

What John the Revelator calls "*His Seat*," Daniel the Prophet calls "*The Sanctuary of Strength*." Here, "strength" is often translated as fort or fortified. Thus, this phrase alludes to the Sanctuary of the Fortified City—Rome. One of the reasons the Bishops of Rome claimed to have authority over all other Bishops was because they were the bishops presiding over the "Eternal City."[42]

What Daniel calls the "*taking away of the daily*," John calls "*great authority*." Both phrases refer to how the true church was substituted for a false church.

---

[42] Shotwell, James T.; Loomis, Louise Ropes (1927). The See of Peter. Records of civilization, sources and studies. New York: Columbia University Press, pp. 217, 218, 220

This authority also replaced the Sabbath with Sunday, instituted image worship, and added other false doctrines.

If you read my book, *The Clear and Present Truth of the Daily Sacrifice*, you will understand the Daily Sacrifice is not a sacrifice. The word "sacrifice" was erroneously added to the text by the Bible translators. The Daily simply means continual. The Continual was the continuation of Israel under the New Covenant—also known as the New Testament Church. The Daily (true Christianity) was taken away and replaced by the Abomination of Desolation.

If you read my book, *The Clear and Present Truth of the Abomination of Desolation*, you will realize that an Abomination occurs when Satan's forces invade God's territory. A physical Abomination of Desolation took place when the Romans invaded Jerusalem in 70 AD and destroyed the city; however, Daniel here is describing a spiritual invasion. In 538 AD, God's Church was spiritually invaded by Satan's forces. Paganism joined Christianity, and the desolation of the Christian Church ensued.

The official transition from Pagan Rome to Papal Rome occurred after the Pope was given power from Justinian's edict, after the Bishop of Rome moved back to the Eternal City, and after Justinian's 90-day ultimatum in which he "...*published edicts in 538 AD compelling all to join the Catholic church in 90 days or leave the empire.*" Dr. N Summerbell, History of the Christian Church, p. 311.

The Papacy now had the *arms*, it presided over the *sanctuary of strength*, and it replaced the *Daily* with the *Abomination of Desolation*.

- The Dark Ages -

Daniel 11:32 - And such as do wickedly against the covenant shall he corrupt by flatteries: but the people that do know their God shall be strong, and do exploits.

According to Summerbell, Emperor Justinian patronized Catholics but persecuted Christians. He also confiscated all non-Catholic Churches and gave their property to the Catholics.[43]

Prophecy revealed that flatteries would corrupt the Christians who converted to Roman Catholicism, and that's precisely what Rome did through Emperor Justinian. We should also know that God retained a remnant of believers who would not bow their knees to "Baal." Even though the true Church had to go underground due to fierce persecution, the Bible declared that these people *knew their God*, and their faith remained *strong*.

- 1260 years of persecution -

Daniel 11:33 - And they that understand among the people shall instruct many: yet they shall fall by the sword, and by flame, by captivity, and by spoil, many days.

The remnant of believers who understood the scriptures and whose eyes were open to the Papacy's deceptions became heretics in the eyes of Catholics.

During this persecution, God raised up individuals such as John Wycliffe, Huss and Jerome,

---

[43] Summerbell, N. (Nicholas), 1816-1889: History of the Christian Church from its establishment by Christ to A.D. 1871 Cincinnati : Published at the Office of the Christian Pulpit, 1873,

Martin Luther and Zwingli, Cranmer, Latimer, Knox, John, and Charles Wesley, and a host of others who *understood* the truth and *instructed many*. Groups such as the Waldensians and the Huguenots, among others, refused to let Rome control the dictates of their conscience and the church survived while underground.

Daniel revealed to us that these individuals would *fall by the sword, and by flame, by captivity, and by spoil, many days.*

Daniel 12:7 also revealed to us that the *many days* of persecution was 1260 years when it says, *it shall be for a time, times, and an half; and when he shall have accomplished to scatter the power of the holy people, all these things shall be finished.*

Time = 360 years,
Times = 720 years,
Half of time = 180 years

If you add these together, it equals 1,260 years. This was the length of time the Christians, who *knew their God* and were *strong*, had to withstand the persecution of the Dark Ages.

1517 AD

Luther's theses were nailed to the door of All Saints' Church, Wittenberg, Germany

- The Protestant Reformation -

Daniel 11:34 - Now when they shall fall, they shall be holpen with a little help: but many shall cleave to them with flatteries.

1517 AD is the year most scholars point to as the beginning of the Protestant Reformation. Martin Luther nailed 95 theses to the door of the Church in Wittenberg, Germany, in protest of the sins of the Catholic church, and the movement took a foothold. The Reformation was the *help* that true Christianity was given during the Dark Ages of Papal supremacy. Unfortunately, some of the kings remained faithful to the flatteries given to them by the Papacy, and they attempted to destroy the Protestant movement. Regarding these flatteries, Ellen White makes the following statement:

> "Rome was not idle. Her emissaries hastened to Germany to congratulate the new emperor, Charles the Fifth, and by their **flatteries**, false representations, and protests, influenced him to employ his power against the Reformation." *The Signs of the Times August 2, 1883*

Daniel 11:35 - And some of them of understanding shall fall, to try them, and to purge, and to make them white, even to the time of the end: because it is yet for a time appointed.

Those who followed Martin Luther's protest and *understood* the truth were known as Protestant Christians. Daniel prophesied that these individuals would be *tried* and *purged* and *made white*. According to history, many of these individuals were placed on trial and executed; however, as martyrs, they were also made spotless in God's eyes. Daniel revealed that this period of persecution would not end until 1798 AD, which was the *time of the end*. Until then, the saints would have to maintain their patience.

1798 AD

- The fall of the Papacy -

Daniel 11:36 - And the king shall do according to his will; and

he shall exalt himself, and magnify himself above every god, and shall speak marvellous things against the God of gods, and shall prosper till the indignation be accomplished: for that that is determined shall be done.

In the second letter to the Thessalonians, the Apostle Paul exposed the "Man of sin" as the one *who opposeth and exalteth himself above all that is called God, or that is worshipped; so that he as God sitteth in the temple of God, shewing himself that he is God.* 2 Thessalonians 2:4. Interestingly, Daniel here speaks about a power that would *exalt himself*. It is evident that Daniel and Paul were referring to the same Papal power that ruled the Dark Ages.

For 1260 years, the Papacy reigned supreme. However, in this supremacy, we must understand that, at times, the Popes were subject to the will of the Emperor. There were also times when multiple Popes reigned simultaneously and fought for control. Through all of that, the Papacy still dominated the church, and these sinful men often exalted their authority above the authority of the God of heaven. Regarding this self-exaltation, Ellen White says,

> "It is one of the leading doctrines of Romanism that the pope is the visible head of the universal church of Christ, invested with supreme authority over bishops and pastors in all parts of the world. More than this, the pope has arrogated the very titles of Deity. He styles himself "Lord God the Pope," assumes infallibility, and demands that all men pay him homage." *1888 The Great Controversy, p. 50.*

The Papacy prospered for over a thousand years until the *indignation* was *accomplished*. God determined that date would be February 10, 1798 AD, when General Louis-Alexandre Berthier, under orders from Napoleon, marched to Rome and demanded Pope Pius VI relinquish his temporal authority. Upon his refusal, the Pontiff was imprisoned where he ultimately died. Another Pope was appointed in 1800, but the Papacy's power and influence never recovered from that day. What God had *determined* was *done*.

Chapter 6

THE OTTOMAN EMPIRE

Kingdom Profile
The Islamic superpower that rose to dominance in the Dark Ages and conquered much of the Southeastern Byzantine territory.

- **Period of dominance**: 1299 AD - 1922 AD
- **Popular ruler(s)**: Suleiman the Magnificent
- **Modern location**: Turkey
- **Notable activity**: Conquered Byzantium
- **Location in Daniel 11**: Verses 37-39

- The Ottoman Empire -

Daniel 11:37 - Neither shall he regard the God of his fathers, nor the desire of women, nor regard any god: for he shall magnify himself above all.

Considering the Papal power lost steam in 1798 AD, the next three verses of Daniel 11 seem to prepare us for the world's grand finale by briefly focusing on a power that came into prominence during Papal supremacy—the Ottoman Empire. Originating from Turkey and absorbing much of the Byzantine territory, the Ottoman Empire controlled Southeastern Europe, Western Asia, and Northern Africa. It should be clear to you that the Ottoman Empire was the King of the South!

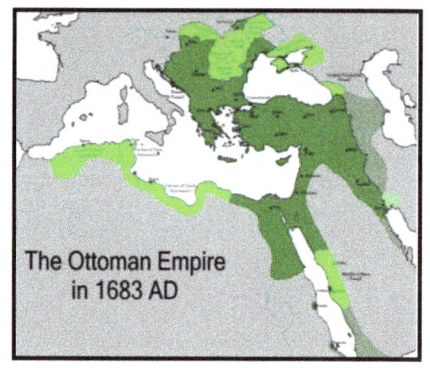
The Ottoman Empire in 1683 AD

The Turkish Ottomans were Muslim; however, long before they converted to Islam, there was a significant Christian presence among the Turkish people. Some may not realize that when John the Revelator wrote to *"the seven churches which are in Asia"* (Revelation 1:11), this was actually Asia-Minor, which is present-day Turkey. Even though the Ottomans have been Muslim for many generations, it can be said, that Jehovah was *the God of their fathers.*

Because this verse deals with deities, I believe *"the desire of women"* is better interpreted as *"...the woman who is desired."* And when we look at female deities, our focus is quickly placed on the most notable one—The Queen of Heaven. Regarding this goddess, Jeremiah 7:18 says, *"The children gather wood, and the fathers kindle the fire, and the women knead their dough, to make cakes to the queen of heaven, and to pour out drink offerings unto other gods, that they may provoke me to anger."*

Although the Queen of Heaven had a history with the Jews, the problem with this theory is that during the time of the Ottoman Empire, the worship of Pagan deities had vastly declined. It is somewhat strange for the angel to make a point about this Pagan deity when much of the known world had converted to Christianity or Islam. Knowing the timeframe that this prophecy pointed to, we understand that there was a woman who was called blessed during the dark ages. This woman was revered to the point that she was elevated to a goddess-like status by the Papacy. It should be clear to you at this point, that the woman who was desired in this prophecy was Mary, the mother of the Messiah. And even though Catholics deny worshipping her, it's no coincidence that they also call her the Queen of Heaven. And when we see people bowing and praying to statues of her in their churches, it's easy to see that this prophecy is referring to Mary as the woman who was desired.

As an Islamic world power, the Ottoman Empire was different from most conquering nations because it did not force those it conquered to convert to Islam. As a matter of fact, the Ottomans established the millet system, which allowed each religious group to maintain their own faith, have their own spiritual leader, and rule themselves according to their individual laws.[44]

Due to the fact the Ottomans weren't inclined to convert those they conquered, the Ottoman Empire

---

[44] Kia, Mehrdad. Daily Life in the Ottoman Empire. United Kingdom: ABC-CLIO, 2011, p 117.

essentially had *no regard for* Jehovah—*the God of their fathers,* or Mary—*the desired woman, nor a regard* for *any god* of those it conquered. This was how the Ottoman Empire *magnified* and grew—because they received less resistance than other nations that forced religious conversions upon those it conquered.

- The god of the Ottomans -

Daniel 11:38 - But in his estate shall he honour the God of forces: and a god whom his fathers knew not shall he honour with gold, and silver, and with precious stones, and pleasant things.

Unlike the Byzantine Empire, the god who was honored in Asia-Minor was known as the *god of forces.*

In the original language, the word "forces" is also translated as a fortress, a fortified place, or a fenced city.[45] If we contemplate why cities needed to be fortified, there is really one reason—for times of war. Cities were usually fortified as a defensive measure against potential attacks from their enemies. And though other religions and ethnicities have also fought wars, we must remember what God specifically said about Ishmael, the father of the Islamic nations:

> "And he will be a wild man; his
> hand will be against every man,
> and every man's hand against him;
> and he shall dwell in the presence
> of all his brethren." Genesis 16:12

Even though the Turkish-Ottomans were not descendants of Ishmael, they shared the same faith as

---

[45] "H4581 - ma`owz - Strong's Hebrew Lexicon (KJV)." Blue Letter Bible. Accessed 15 Dec, 2020. https://www.blueletterbible.org//lang/lexicon/lexicon.cfm?Strongs=H4581&t=KJV

Ishmael's descendants. According to Genesis 16:12, Ishmael and his descendants will constantly be at war with others, and others will constantly be at war with them. We can now understand why Daniel declared a people historically involved in Jihad as worshipping the *God of fortresses*.

Considering Christianity was part of the early Turkish culture, and Islam wasn't established until the seventh century, it makes sense that Allah is the god that their ancestors *knew not*.

Allah was the *god of forces* who was *honoured* by the Ottomans within the Turkish *estate*.

Similar to Catholic structures, the Muslims also honour their god with gold, *silver, and precious stones*.

1918 AD – 1923 AD

– The end of the Ottoman Empire –

Daniel 11:39 – Thus shall he do in the most strong holds with a strange god, whom he shall acknowledge and increase with glory: and he shall cause them to rule over many, and shall divide the land for gain.

The religion of Islam began in the seventh century, shortly after the rise of the Papacy. Interestingly, the Islamic superpower known as the Ottoman Empire began to decline soon after the Papacy fell in 1798 AD. It is almost as if the King of the North (Papal power) has a parallel antagonist (Islam) that rises to power whenever the Papal power becomes too strong and then recedes as the Papacy's authority declines. But I digress. "*Strange*" in the original language of the Bible can also mean foreign. Even though the Ottomans *ruled over many*, the god of Islam was still *foreign* to those they conquered. After World War I, the vast conglomeration of territories that formed the Ottoman Empire was divided into several new states by the British and French.[46] According to scripture, the Ottoman Empire was *divided for gain*. Islam has not produced a superpower since that time.

---

[46] Roderic H. Davison; Review "From Paris to Sèvres: The Partition of the Ottoman Empire at the Peace Conference of 1919–1920" by Paul C. Helmreich in Slavic Review, Vol. 34, No. 1 (Mar. 1975), pp. 186–187

Chapter 7

THE UNITED STATES OF AMERICA

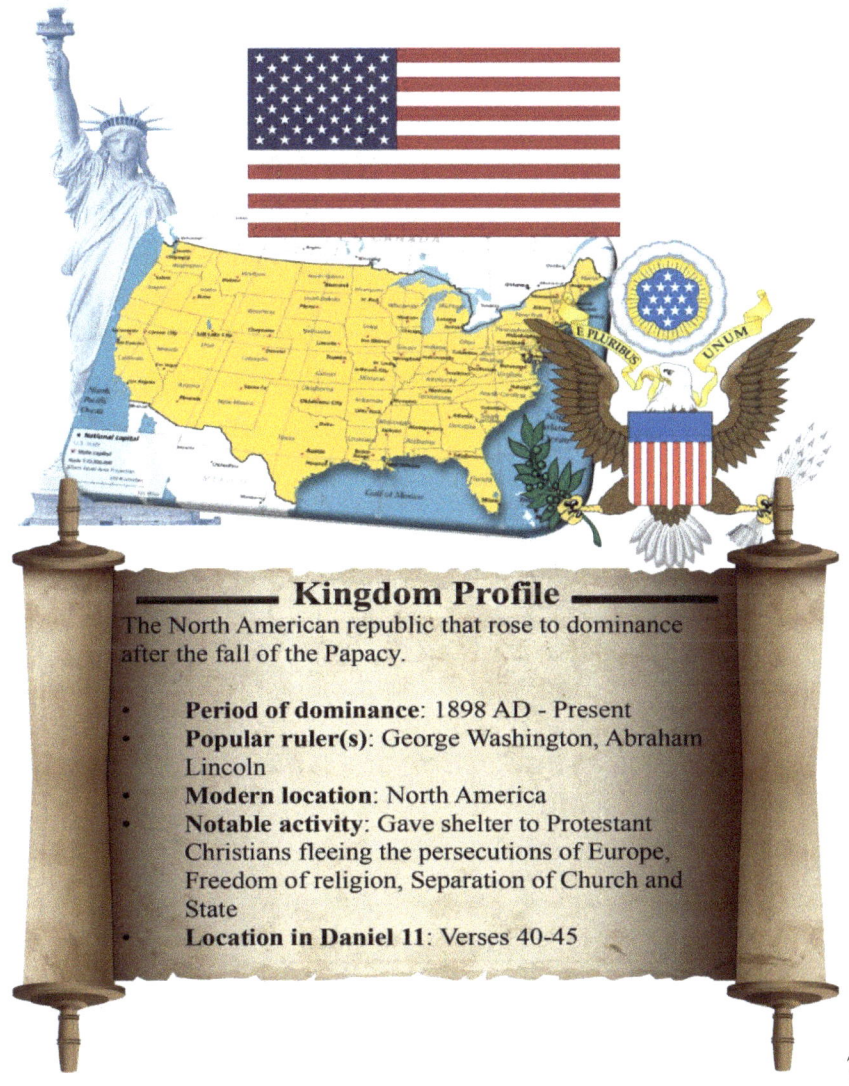

Kingdom Profile

The North American republic that rose to dominance after the fall of the Papacy.

- **Period of dominance**: 1898 AD - Present
- **Popular ruler(s)**: George Washington, Abraham Lincoln
- **Modern location**: North America
- **Notable activity**: Gave shelter to Protestant Christians fleeing the persecutions of Europe, Freedom of religion, Separation of Church and State
- **Location in Daniel 11**: Verses 40-45

Some who are reading this chapter may be curious to understand how I determined the United States is part of the prophetic lens of Daniel 11. For an in-depth study on this subject, I suggest you read another book I wrote titled—*The Clear and Present Truth of 666*. However, in order for this chapter to make sense, let me briefly explain the rationale behind my position.

Daniel 11 closes with America as the last world power even though other prophetic chapters of Daniel end with the Roman Empire. I am comfortable with this view because of one reason—America *is* part of the Roman Empire. Obviously, I am not suggesting that America is a Roman province; however, prophetically, America is part of Rome. Let me explain how we determine this to be true:

When we look at the components of spiritual Babylon, Revelation 16:19 helps us understand that *the great city was divided into three parts*. We also know that these three parts are the Dragon, the Beast, and the False Prophet (Revelation 16:13). According to the Seventh-Day Adventist Bible Commentary, The Dragon represents Spiritualism (Pagan Rome), the Beast represents Catholicism (Papal Rome), and the False Prophet represents Apostate Protestantism (America).[47] Now remember, these components are the three divisions of Mystical Babylon. A three-part union is what we call a trinity. This same trinity is what Ellen White called a *"threefold union."*[48] She also declared that these three entities are part of *"the same family."*[49] So even though they are three distinct entities,

---

[47] Nichol, Francis D. 1953. The Seventh-Day Adventist Bible commentary; Washington: Review and Herald Pub. Association. p. 847
[48] White, Ellen G. 1950. The great controversy between Christ and Satan. Mountain View, Calif: Pacific Press Pub. Association. p.588
[49] White, Ellen G. 1950. The great controversy between Christ and Satan. Mountain View, Calif: Pacific Press Pub. Association. p.680

prophetically, they are one. The Dragon, the Beast, and the False Prophet are one power divided into three sections. This tells us that Pagan Rome was revived as Papal Rome and Papal Rome was revived under Protestant America. America is essentially the continuation of the Papal power. Regarding America, John the Revelator says, "*he is the eighth, and is of the seven...*" Revelation 17:11. If the Papacy was the seventh, then America, which came after the Papacy, is the eighth. This confirms America (the eighth) is part of Papal Rome (the seventh). So even though Daniel 11 ends with the United States of America, in reality, it still ends under the dispensation of the Roman Empire.

2001 AD

– September 11th Terrorist Attack on America –

Daniel 11:40 - And at the time of the end shall the king of the south push at him: and the king of the north shall come against him like a whirlwind, with chariots, and with horsemen, and with many ships; and he shall enter into the countries, and shall overflow and pass over.

The time of the end refers to the period of earth's history after the fall of the Papacy in 1798 AD.[50] Even though this period of time began in 1798, we must be careful not to restrict the time of the end solely to that year. Verse 40 brings us to a startling moment in earth's history. On September 11, 2001, a group of Muslim terrorists

---

[50] White, Ellen G. 1950. The Great Controversy between Christ and Satan 1888: The Conflict of the Ages in the Christian Dispensation. Mountain View, Calif: Pacific Press Pub. Association. p. 356

hijacked multiple commercial airplanes and crashed them into American targets, including the World Trade Center towers in New York City. These Muslim extremists came from Saudi Arabia, the United Arab Emirates, Lebanon, and Egypt—all territories of the former Ottoman Empire.[51] However, we also recognize that they are also currently part of the Arab League. In this way, we can see that prophetically these Islamic territories are still considered the King of the South! And their attack on the United States of America was the event Daniel referred to as the King of the South *pushing at him* (the King of the North).

After the Islamic extremists *pushed*, America retaliated and *came against* multiple Middle Eastern countries like a *whirlwind* with their tanks, soldiers, and

the War on Terror. Even though the primary focus of this war was on Iraq and Afghanistan, the War on Terror's overall focus was Muslim countries in the Middle East—the King of the South's territory. The United States and its allies entered these countries, toppled regimes, and killed dictators.

---

[51] Only the west coast of modern Saudi Arabia belonged to the Ottoman Empire.

The Future

- The war escalates -

Daniel 11:41 - He shall enter also into the glorious land, and many countries shall be overthrown: but these shall escape out of his hand, even Edom, and Moab, and the chief of the children of Ammon.

As of today, the War on Terror has subsided and American troops are being sent back home. However, according to verse 41, the war between the King of the North (America) and the King of the South (Islamic countries) is not over. In the future, a conflict between these two powers will escalate, and America will enter the region of the Middle East known as Palestine or, as Daniel calls it—*the glorious land.*

Assuming America and Israel are still allies in the future, we have one logical reason why America would find it necessary to enter the glorious land: In the future, a confederacy of Muslim nations will attack Israel. This attack on Israel will not be the typical small missile strikes we've seen coming from Palestinian militants in the past; this will be a full-scale attack against Israel to which the United States of America will respond by entering the region.

Daniel then declares that Edom, Moab, and the chief of the children of Ammon will escape this onslaught. Scriptures reveal that the Israelites initially encountered these three heathen tribes during their journey from Egypt to the promised land.[52] According to the Bible, the Israelites were not allowed to pass

---

[52] Edomites were the ancestors of Esau. Ammon and Moab were the results of the incestuous relationship between Lot and his daughters.

through their territory, and God forbade Israel from troubling them:

> "And command thou the people, saying, Ye are to pass through the coast of your brethren the children of **Esau**,[53] which dwell in Seir; and they shall be afraid of you: take ye good heed unto yourselves therefore: Meddle not with them; for I will not give you of their land, no, not so much as a foot breadth; because I have given mount Seir unto Esau for a possession." Deuteronomy 2:4-5

> "And the LORD said unto me, Distress not the **Moabites**, neither contend with them in battle: for I will not give thee of their land for a possession; because I have given Ar unto the children of Lot for a possession." Deuteronomy 2:9

> "And when thou comest nigh over against the children of **Ammon**, distress them not, nor meddle with them: for I will not give thee of the land of the children of Ammon any possession; because I have given it unto the children of Lot for a possession." Deuteronomy 2:19

According to the Bible, the children of Ammon, Moab, and Edom were given their land directly from God, and Israel was not allowed to war against them in order to take their territory for themselves. Modern-day maps reveal that Edom, Moab, and Ammon were

---
[53] Edomites were descendants of Esau.

Today, Ammon, Moab, and Edom would be located in the country of Jordan

situated in the same region of the world that the country of Jordan is located today.

According to the end-time prophecy of Daniel 11, when the United States military and its allies come against the glorious land, they will honor the command that God gave Israel in Deuteronomy 2 and refrain from attacking the country of Jordan (most likely at the request of Evangelical leaders). In this fashion, *Edom, Moab, and the chief of the children of Ammon escape out of his* (America's) *hand.*

We must also be careful to point out that Daniel did not say "Ammon" by itself. He said, "*the chief of the children of Ammon.*" In the original language, chief means first in rank or principal thing. Here, it is applicable to point out that the chief city of this country was called Rabbath Ammon, which is the site of the modern city of Amman—Jordan's capital. The chief of the children of Ammon most likely refers to the capital of Jordan and the officials situated there.

- America attacks the original King of the South -

Daniel 11:42 - He shall stretch forth his hand also upon the countries: and the land of gypt shall not escape.

Daniel provides us further insight into this apocalyptic clash between the King of the North and the King of the South.

During this incursion, the Islamic nations south of Israel will be brought into the conflict, including Egypt—the original King of the South. The United States armed forces and its allies will attack this territory, and Egypt will fall along with the surrounding Islamic countries.

- America takes control of North Africa's minerals -

Daniel 11:43 - But he shall have power over the treasures of gold and of silver, and over all the precious things of Egypt: and the Libyans and the Ethiopians shall be at his steps.

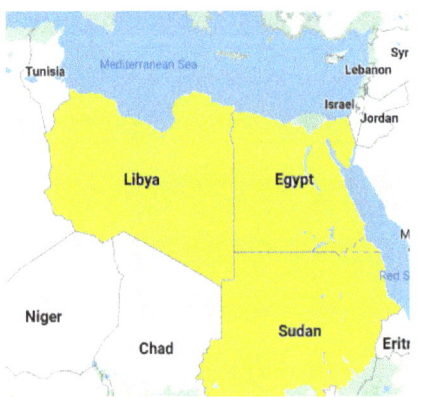

The incursion of verse 43 appears to focus on this region of north Africa.

After Iraq was toppled in 2003, the United States took control of Iraq's biggest asset—their oil. In the coming conflict between the North and South, Egypt will be relegated to a similar arrangement with the western superpower. However, it appears that this arrangements focus will be the countries precious metals.

The United States of America will control the economy of Egypt, which will include its gold and precious metals.

Daniel continues by revealing that both African nations that border Egypt will follow in the *footsteps* of Egypt. Understand that the Ethiopia of Bible times is geographically different from our modern-day Ethiopia. What the Bible called Ethiopia would be considered

Southern Egypt and Northern Sudan today.⁵⁴ According to the Bible, Egypt's neighbors, the *Libyans* and *Ethiopians* (Sudanese), will suffer the same fate as Egypt.

Interestingly, the Islamic uprising of the early 2010s (also known as the Arab Spring) involved Egypt and Libya—two of the nations mentioned in verse 43. Other countries involved in the demonstrations and protests included Yemen, Syria, Bahrain, and Tunisia. Is it possible that these countries will also become involved in the final war between the King of the North and the King of the South?

- Middle Eastern nations join the conflict -

Daniel 11:44 - But tidings out of the east and out of the north shall trouble him: therefore he shall go forth with great fury to destroy, and utterly to make away many.

While the US and its allies are involved in a full-scale conflict with the powers of the South, other Islamic powers will gain the attention of America and its allies. Daniel reveals that during this conflict, there will be news out of the East and the North. Some would say the east and the north represent North Korea and Russia—which is plausible; however, if we are to take Daniel 11 literally, then the Bible has already provided us the exact location of this north and eastern region.

If you recall, chapter three revealed that Seleucus I Nicator was the king of the eastern division of the divided Greek Empire. However, we should also recall that Seleucus would go on to conquer the territory of

---

[54] "Ethiopians (Cushites) ." New Catholic Encyclopedia. . Encyclopedia.com. (December 19, 2020). https://www.encyclopedia.com/religion/encyclopedias-almanacs-transcripts-and-maps/ethiopians-cushites

Lysimachus at the Battle of Corupedium. In case you forgot, Lysimachus was the then king of Asia Minor, which was in the north. Once Seleucus conquered Asia Minor, he became the king of the east and the north! And now it should be clear that the territory that was formerly part of the Seleucid Empire is the same part of the world that tidings will come out from and capture America's attention.

Today, these directions will essentially point us to Turkey and the Middle East!

If our understanding of this prophecy is correct, this would indicate that during America's conflict with North Africa, we will see Turkey in the north, and countries such as Syria, Iran, Iraq, Pakistan, and Afghanistan in the east be the powers to likely gain America's full attention during this end-time conflict.

We do not have to guess how this conflict will conclude; the scripture says *he* (the United States) *shall go forth with great fury to destroy, and utterly to make away many.*

- The Papacy is relocated to Jerusalem -

Daniel 11:45 - And he shall plant the tabernacles of his palace between the seas in the glorious holy mountain; yet he shall come to his end, and none shall help him.

It is important to understand that the last five verses of Daniel refer to war. If you do not believe me, then believe the words of Ellen White, who made the following comment on Daniel 11:

> "The world is stirred with the **spirit of war**. The prophecy of the **eleventh chapter of Daniel has nearly reached its complete fulfillment**. Soon the scenes of trouble spoken of in the prophecies will take place." *Testimonies for the Church*, vol.9, p. 14.

Notice, Ellen White revealed that the end of Daniel 11 is about the *spirit of war* within the world. It is this *spirit of war* that indicates the prophecies of Daniel 11 have nearly reached their fulfillment. This is not the only statement she would make regarding war at the end of the world:

> "The world is becoming more and more lawless. **Soon great trouble will arise among the nations—trouble that will not cease until Jesus comes.**" *The Review and Herald*, February 11, 1904.

We must be careful not to force prophecy to fit our own narratives. The last five verses of Daniel should not be taken as a metaphor between good and evil. The last five verses of Daniel do not refer to the Mark of the Beast, the Church, or persecution. Daniel 11:40-45 gives us a panoramic view of what will be happening among the nations right before probation closes—and that is war.

Verse 45 relates to the outcome of this final conflict between nations. This outcome is important because it leads to the events that occur after Michael stands up in Daniel 12.

Up to this point, I have not mentioned any involvement of the Papacy in this final conflict between nations. However, make no mistake, the Papacy will be behind the scenes pulling the strings as they have historically done.

Verse 45 says, "*And he shall plant the tabernacles of his palace between the seas in the glorious holy mountain...*" We do not have the guess what the glorious holy mountain is, Daniel 9:16 reveals this to us:

> "I beseech thee, let thine anger and thy fury be turned away from thy city **Jerusalem, thy holy mountain...**"

Even though we don't have all the details of Jerusalem's outcome, it appears that this final war between the United States and the Middle East paves the way for the Papacy to move its headquarters into Jerusalem. The degree of power and control the Vatican will have over Jerusalem has not been revealed, but we know that somehow, *his* (the Papacy's) *tabernacle will be planted between the seas in the glorious holy mountain* (Jerusalem).

Now, if you will allow me to connect the prophetic dots, you will see why the Papacy needs Jerusalem, and you will see how this will set the world up for the close of probation and the Time of Trouble.

- The End of the World -

I am going to take some liberties in what I'm about to explain. Please understand that I am merely connecting the dots of end-time events. I may be entirely off regarding the interpretation of these final moments; however, if I am correct, then God is showing us exactly what events to expect from a global perspective before the Time of Trouble.

~ ~ ~ ~ ~

Once the Vatican is firmly planted in Jerusalem, this will produce anger from the remaining Muslim countries (and possibly other non-Muslim countries). The world will be divided on this issue, but the united Muslim countries (or as I call them Ottoman 2.0) will retaliate in an attempt to destroy the King of the North (the Papacy and the United States) and take Jerusalem.

This final war that began with an attack on the United States will culminate in a war for Jerusalem, the *glorious holy mountain*.

To give you better context, I believe that Daniel 11:40-45 relates to the *wars and rumors of wars* declared in Matthew 24. Both chapters are referring to the final conflict between the nations.

Daniel 11:40 says	**Matthew 24:7 says**
He shall enter also into the glorious land, and many countries shall be overthrown.	*For nation shall rise against nation, and kingdom against kingdom:*

The final war of Daniel 11:40-45 is setting the scene for a false Millennium. However, before we expose this false Millennium, we must first ensure that we have a firm understanding of the true Biblical Millennium.

According to Revelation 20, the Millennium is a thousand-year period that begins after the Second

Coming of Christ. At the Second Coming, the wicked will be destroyed (2 Thessalonians 1:7-9), and those who are saved will be taken to heaven to spend with the Lord (1 Thessalonians 4:17). During this thousand-year period, Satan and his angels will be bound to the earth, which will also be known as the bottomless pit. At the end of the Millennium, Jesus will bring New Jerusalem and the saints down from heaven; and the wicked will then be raised from the dead to see the city. It is not long afterward that Satan will rally the wicked to attack the city. On this event, John the Revelator says,

> "And shall go out to deceive the nations which are in the four quarters of the earth, Gog and Magog, to gather them together to battle: the number of whom is as the sand of the sea. And they went up on the breadth of the earth, and compassed the camp of the saints about, and the beloved city: and fire came down from God out of heaven, and devoured them." Revelation 20:8-9

Now, I need you to see this vision. We see Jerusalem with the saints inside its walls, and Satan, along with the wicked coming against the city, resulting in fire coming down from heaven devouring them. This is the true Millennium; however, you must understand there is also a false Millennium. Notice Ellen White's description of this great deception:

> "They declared that they had the truth, that miracles were among them, that angels from heaven talked with them and walked with them, that great power, and signs and wonders were performed

among them, and this was the **Temporal Millennium**, which they had been expecting so long." *Maranatha* p. 209

Those who adhere to the temporal Millennium differ on this doctrine's details, but they generally agree that there will be a seven-year tribulation period followed by a thousand years of peace while Christ reigns on earth. With that understanding, we can connect the dots of end-time events:

After the King of the North receives Jerusalem, and a Muslim confederacy comes against the Papacy/ US in Jerusalem, the stage will be set for the temporal or false Millennium.

The Evangelical world will be under the impression that this final war against Jerusalem is the seven-year tribulation. They will be deceived into believing the Muslims are the wicked who will be as *the sand of the sea* coming up to *compass the camp of the saints about the beloved city* of Jerusalem. However, Evangelicals know that in order for this to be the Millennium of the Scriptures, fire must come down from God out of heaven. So, while the Muslims are coming up against Jerusalem, and the Evangelicals are under false assumptions, Satan will prepare the world for his crowning act by personating Christ and bringing fire down from heaven. Regarding these two events, the Bible reveals the following:

> "And no marvel; for Satan himself is transformed into an angel of light." 2Corinthians 11:14

> "And he doeth great wonders, so that he maketh fire come down from heaven on

the earth in the sight of men." Revelation 13:13

Regarding this spectacle, Ellen White says,

> "It is the lying wonders of the devil that will take the world captive, and he will cause fire to come down from heaven in the sight of men. He is to work miracles, and this wonderful, miracle-working power is to sweep in the whole world." *Last Day Events*, p. 167

Matthew 24:5,23-24 confirms that during this end-time conflict, the world will experience false Christs. I have no doubt this is Satan himself. The reason Satan will appear as an *angel of light* is to deceive the world into worshipping him.

Now let me ask you a question: If Jesus (the real Jesus) appeared on earth today, where might He go? He would probably go to America as the world's current Superpower. I would also guess that He would also visit many of the Christian-majority countries. However, at some point, wouldn't you expect Him to go to Jerusalem? What do you think the world would expect Jesus to do?

When Satan personates Christ, he will show up in Jerusalem, where the Papacy and US leaders will greet him. The Papacy, acting as a forerunner for "Christ," will help facilitate this last great deception. The Dragon (Satan), the Beast (Catholicism), and the False Prophet (corrupt Protestant Christianity) will all be working together in these final scenes.

As the US-led forces attempt to defend the region, the unified Muslim armies will come against Jerusalem. However, before a missile is fired or a trigger is pulled, Satan will make his grand entrance. Deceiving the world into believing he is Christ, he will call fire down from heaven and destroy the federation of Muslim forces. Once this occurs, the world will believe the "tribulation" has ended.

It is imperative you understand that there are two scenarios in which fire comes down from heaven in the last days. Notice how John presents both of them:

> "And he doeth great wonders, so that **he maketh fire come down from heaven on the earth in the sight of men**." Revelation 13:13

> "And they went up on the breadth of the earth, and compassed the camp of the saints about, and the beloved city: **and fire came down from God out of heaven, and devoured them**." Revelation 20:9

It should be understood that both fires are sent down from heaven; however, the first fire comes from Satan, and the second fire comes from God. The most significant difference we must understand is *when* these fires occur.

Satan will bring fire down from heaven *before* the Millennium; God will send fire down from heaven *after* the Millennium. This alone should reveal how important it is for the world to understand the true Millennium.

Once Satan devours the Islamic forces, the "conversion" of the world will begin. In order to help this global conversion, Satan's demons will begin transforming themselves into heathen deities to bring the non-Christian world into harmony. On this great deception, Ellen White says,

> "As we near the close of time, there will be greater and still greater external parade of heathen power; **heathen deities** will manifest their signal power and will exhibit themselves before the cities of the world..." *Manuscript 139, 1903*

Is it possible Satan's demons will personate Mohammed and Buddha to bring the Non-Christian world into harmony? What if one of Satan's demons portrays himself as the Anti-Christ in order to deceive the Christian world into believing Satan is the real Jesus? We may not know the specifics, but we do know that Satan will deceive the world into worshiping him.

As Satan and his demons bring the world into harmony, this will begin what Ellen White called the temporal Millennium. This is when the world will be "converted" and be at "peace." Understand, the temporal Millennium is "*when*" the people will say "*peace and safety.*"[55] However, some may not realize that after they say, "*Peace and safety,*" then "*sudden destruction cometh upon them.*" Regarding this time of peace Ellen White says the following:

> "I was shown the inhabitants of the earth in the utmost confusion. War, bloodshed, privation, want, famine, and pestilence were abroad in the land.... My attention was then called from the scene. **There seemed to be a little time of peace**. Once more the inhabitants of the earth were presented before me; and again everything was in the utmost confusion. Strife, war, and bloodshed, with famine

---
[55] 1 Thessalonians 5:3

and pestilence, raged everywhere. Other nations were engaged in this war and confusion. War caused famine. Want and bloodshed caused pestilence. And then men's hearts failed them for fear, "and for looking after those things which are coming on the earth." *Christian Service* p. 55

Notice Ellen White talked about the inhabitants of the earth being in the utmost confusion. I believe that this is a clear reference to the war at the end of Daniel 11. Now notice she then says there will be a time of peace! This time of peace is the temporal Millennium! Then, while the world is basking in this false peace and safety known as the temporal Millennium, utmost confusion comes in again! The question is—what brings this utmost confusion amid the temporal Millennium? Notice what Matthew 24 says will happen after the wars and rumors of wars:

> "...and there shall be **famines**, and **pestilences**, and **earthquakes**, in divers places." Matthew 24:7

Disrupting this time of peace and safety, there will be an exponential increase in natural disasters. The world will be confused because they will be under the impression that peace and harmony will bring these disasters to an end. Ellen White provides us with further insight on what happens next:

> "And then the great deceiver will persuade men that those who serve God are causing these evils. The class that have provoked the displeasure of Heaven will charge all

their troubles upon those whose obedience to God's commandments is a perpetual reproof to transgressors. It will be declared that men are offending God by the violation of the Sunday sabbath; that this sin has brought calamities which will not cease until Sunday observance shall be strictly enforced; and that those who present the claims of the fourth commandment, thus destroying reverence for Sunday, are troublers of the people, preventing their restoration to divine favor and temporal prosperity." *The Great Controversy* p.590

"Those who honor the Bible Sabbath will be denounced as enemies of law and order, as breaking down the moral restraints of society, causing anarchy and corruption, and calling down the judgments of God upon the earth...They will be accused of disaffection toward the government. Ministers who deny the obligation of the divine law will present from the pulpit the duty of yielding obedience to the civil authorities as ordained of God." *The Great Controversy* p. 592

"Men in responsible positions... will point to calamities on land and sea—to the storms of wind, the floods, the earthquakes, the destruction by fire—as judgments indicating God's displeasure because Sunday is not sacredly observed.

These calamities will increase more and more, one disaster will follow close upon the heels of another; and those who make void the law of God will point to the few who are keeping the Sabbath of the fourth commandment as the ones who are bringing wrath upon the world." *The Southern Watchman, June 28, 1904.*

Ladies and Gentlemen, James 2:10 says, "*For whosoever shall keep the whole law, and yet offend in one point, he is guilty of all.*" Satan understands that we are saved by grace (Ephesians 2:8), but he also understands we are judged by our works (Revelation 20:13). While there are multiple Sabbaths throughout the Bible, only one Sabbath was instituted prior to the entrance of sin—that is the seventh-day Sabbath. This is the only Sabbath that was part of the Ten Commandments and is the only Sabbath still binding on humanity today. Satan's plan is to deceive the whole Christian world into replacing the Seventh-day Sabbath with a Sunday Sabbath. Understand, this is more than just going to church on the first day of the week. Satan, who wants to be God, will attempt to establish his own Sabbath day as God did during creation week. This counterfeit Sabbath will be Sunday.

There are good people who do not honor the seventh-day Sabbath because they have yet to see its importance, but during this time, God's law will be clearly understood by every believer on this planet, and we will all have the opportunity to choose truth or error.

Satan's goal is for the world to universally trample upon God's Sabbath and universally keep his replacement Sabbath. The resistance of a few will cause the world to break out in strife and confusion once again. But this time, the strife and confusion will be aimed at those who choose to honor God and His commandments. This is why Revelation 12:17 says, "*And the dragon was wroth with the woman, and went to make war with the remnant of her seed, which keep the commandments of God, and have the testimony of Jesus Christ.*"

Notice the words of the Psalmist, which correctly reveal the sentiment of God's saints during this time:

> "It is time for thee, LORD, to work: for they have made void thy law." Psalms 119:126

Daniel 12 clearly reveals what happens after the time of peace has ended and the world becomes unified against those who would rather die than disobey God's Word:

> "And at that time shall Michael stand up, the great prince which standeth for the children of thy people: and there shall be a time of trouble, such as never was since there was a nation even to that same time: and at that time thy people shall be delivered, every one that shall be found written in the book." Daniel 12:1

When Michael stands up, this is the close of Earth's probation. At this point, the persecution of God's people begins, and the Time of Trouble ensues.

This final persecution will be remarkably similar to the Papal persecution of the Dark Ages; this is why Ellen White says,

> "Much of the history that has taken place in fulfillment of this prophecy [Daniel 11:30-36] will be repeated." *Letter 103, 1904*

Daniel 11:30-36 points to the reign of the Papacy. Whatever persecution was aimed at the true Church in Daniel 11 will be repeated at the true Church in Daniel 12. Regarding this time, the Bible says,

> "Then shall they deliver you up to be afflicted, and shall kill you: and ye shall be hated of all nations for my name's sake." Matthew 24:9

> "...yea, the time cometh, that whosoever killeth you will think that he doeth God service." John 16:2

While the people of God are being persecuted, the seven last plagues will begin falling upon the wicked inhabitants of this earth (Revelation 16). During the plagues, Revelation 16:16 says, "*And he gathered them together into a place called in the Hebrew tongue Armageddon.*" Ladies and Gentlemen, it should be understood that God will not allow His people to be destroyed. Right before the people of God are exterminated, Jesus will be seen coming in the clouds to save them.

After a thousand years in heaven with Christ, Daniel's last words will finally come to fruition, *he* (the Papal and false Christian power) *shall come to his end, and none shall help him.* Regarding this same scene, John the Revelator says,

> "And the **beast** was taken, and with him the **false prophet** that wrought miracles before him, with which he deceived them that had received the mark of the beast, and them that worshipped his image. **These both were cast alive into a lake of fire burning with brimstone.**" Revelation 19:20

Ladies and Gentlemen, it is important that we choose the right side of this conflict. The conflict is not Republican versus Democrat; the conflict is not American versus Muslim. The conflict is good versus evil. On which side will you be found?

Prophecy is important, but without Christ, it has no power to save. While probation is still open for us, now is the time to ask Jesus into our hearts. The line is being drawn in the sand, and we must make our calling and election sure. God has not given us the day or hour of his coming, but I genuinely believe He has given us the Clear and Present Truth of Daniel 11.

THE CLEAR AND PRESENT TRUTH OF
DANIEL 11

TEST YOUR KNOWLEDGE

1. Why didn't God inspire Daniel to directly name all the kings and kingdoms of Daniel 11? (pp. 11-12)

2. Daniel 11 is a detailed account of world powers that encountered God's people. Below, list each world power and the range of verses Daniel 11 assigns to each of them. (Kingdom Profiles)

World Power	Verses

3. Who was the mighty king in verse 3? (p. 30)

4. Greece was ultimately divided by four kings. Who were they, and what compass point did each of them control? (p. 31)

5. Which two kings became the King of the North and the King of the South? (p. 33)

6. Verse 22 says "And with the arms of a flood shall they be overflown from before him, and shall be broken; yea, also the prince of the covenant." What two events are being described? (pp. 46-47)

7. In the 5th century, who became the King of the South? (pp. 48-50)

8. What war strategy did King Genseric employ against the Romans? (p. 52)

9. Which Roman Emperor was against the Holy Covenant? (pp. 53-54)

10. Can you explain how the Emperor of Rome exhibited indignation against the Covenant? (pp. 62-64)

11. What year did the Papacy obtain supremacy? (pp. 65-66)

12. What is the Daily Sacrifice? (pp. 65-66)

13. In Daniel 11, what verses refer to the Protestant Reformation? (pp. 68-69)

14. What year did the Papacy fall? (pp. 71)

15. Which world empire became King of the South during the Papacy's reign? (p. 74)

16. The Ottoman Empire did not have regard for any god. Can you explain how this is possible? (pp. 75-76)

17. How do we determine that the United States is prophetically part of the Roman Empire? (pp. 80-81)

18. In verse 40, it says that the King of the South would push at the King of the North. What event might this be? (pp. 81-82)

19. What country represents Edom, Moab, and Ammon today? (pp. 83-85)

20. What possible reason would Edom, Moab, and the chief of the children of Ammon escape the onslaught coming at the end of time? (p. 85)

21. During the end-time conflict, America gets troubled by tidings from the east and the north. What nations are likely represented by these directions? (pp. 87-88)

22. Match every King of the North to the correlating King of the South.

King of the North	King of the South
Seleucid Empire (Greece)	
Pagan Rome	
Papal Rome	
United States of America	

23. What happens after the war between the nations? (Daniel 12:1)

ANSWERS

1. Why didn't God inspire Daniel to directly name all the kings and kingdoms of Daniel 11? **Daniel 11 is ambiguous so that the kings of the earth would not try to manipulate the prophetic timeline.**

2. Daniel 11 is a detailed account of world powers that encountered God's people. Below, list each world power and the range of verses Daniel 11 assigns to each of them. (Kingdom Profiles)

World Power	Verses
Persia	1-2
Greece	3-16
Pagan Rome	16-30
Papal Rome	30-36
Ottoman Empire	37-39
United States of America	40-45

3. Who was the mighty king in verse 3? **Alexander the Great**

4. Greece was ultimately divided by four kings. Who were they, and what compass point did each of them control?
   Lysimachus - North
   Ptolemy - South
   Seleucus - East
   Cassander - West

5. Which two kings became the King of the North and the King of the South? **Seleucus - North, Ptolemy - South**

6. Verse 22 says, "And with the arms of a flood shall they be overflown from before him, and shall be broken; yea, also the prince of the covenant." What two events are being described? **The Crucifixion of Christ and the destruction of Jerusalem**

7. In the 5th century, who became the King of the South? **The Vandals**

8. What war strategy did King Genseric employ against the Romans? **King Genseric used the captured Roman fleet against his Roman foes.**

9. Which Roman Emperor was against the Holy Covenant? **Justinian I**

10. Can you explain how the Emperor of Rome exhibited indignation against the Covenant? **The Covenant represents God placing His law in our hearts. The Catholic Church made the world believe it had changed God's law, so when Justinian exalted the Bishop of Rome as the authority of the church, this was the catalyst that enabled the world to follow the dictates of Rome.**

11. What year did the Papacy obtain supremacy? **538 AD**

12. What is the Daily Sacrifice? **True Christianity**

13. In Daniel 11, what verses refer to the Protestant Reformation? **Verses 34-35**

14. What year did the Papacy fall? **1798 AD**

15. Which world empire became King of the South during the Papacy's reign? **The Ottoman Empire**

16. The Ottoman Empire did not have regard for any god. Can you explain how this is possible? **The Ottoman Empire never forced religious conversions upon those it conquered.**

17. How do we determine that the United States is prophetically part of the Roman Empire? **The Dragon, Beast, and False Prophet are a trinity. The False Prophet represents false Protestant Christianity, and America is its capital. The False Prophet is prophetically part of the Roman system; therefore, we conclude America is prophetically part of Rome.**

18. In verse 40, it says that the King of the South would push at the King of the North. What event might this be? **The September 11, 2001 attack on the world trade center**

19. What country represents Edom, Moab, and Ammon today? **Jordan**

20. What possible reason would Edom, Moab, and the chief of the children of Ammon escape the onslaught coming at the end of time? **God gave them that specific territory and forbade Israel from bothering them and taking their land. When the US and its allies attack the Middle East, they will leave Jordan alone to comply with God's mandate.**

21. During the end-time conflict, America gets troubled by tidings from the east and the north. What nation does this east and north direction represent? **Turkey, Syria, Iran, Iraq, Pakistan, and Afghanistan**

22. Match every King of the North to the correlating King of the South.

King of the North	King of the South
Seleucid Empire (Greece)	**Ptolemaic Empire (Greece)**
Pagan Rome	**Vandal Nation**
Papal Rome	**Ottoman Empire**
United States of America	**League of Muslim nations**

23. What happens after the war between the nations? **Michael stands up, probation closes, and the time of trouble begins.**

Topical Index

911 terrorist attack, 81

A

Abomination of Desolation, 66
Africa, 48, 49, 52, 57, 59, 74
Alexander the Great, 30, 31,
Ammon, 83, 84, 85
Antiochus Hierax, 35
Antiochus II, 33
Antiochus III, 36, 37, 42
Antiochus IV, 38, 39
Augustus Caesar, 44

B

Babylon, 32, 33, 80, 88
Battle of Cape Bon, 50, 58
Battle of Cartagena, 58
Battle of Corupedium, 32
Berenice, 33, 34

C

Cassander, 31
Catholic, 64, 66, 67, 69, 77, 86
Cleopatra VII, 42, 43
Code of Justinian, 62, 64
Cyrus the Great, 27, 88

D

Daily sacrifice, 65
Darius the Mede, 26
Dark ages, 68, 69, 70, 101
Diadochi Wars, 26, 30, 31
Dragon, 80, 94

E

Edom, 83, 84, 85
Egypt, 31, 32, 34, 35, 36, 38, 39, 42, 43, 47, 83, 85, 86, 87

F

False Prophet, 80, 95,

G

Genseric, 48, 49, 50, 51, 52,
Greece, 27, 30, 31, 32

I

Iraq, 82, 86
Israel, 54, 55, 63, 66, 83, 84, 85, 113

J

Jerusalem, 39, 40, 43, 46, 47, 66, 89, 90, 91, 92, 93, 94
Jesus Christ, 47
Jordan, 84, 85
Judas Maccabeus, 38, 39
Julius Caesar, 11, 42, 43, 44
Justinian the Great, 53

K

King of the North, 21, 31, 36, 39, 40, 42, 47, 77, 82, 83, 85, 87, 91, 93
King of the South, 21, 31, 34, 36, 39, 47, 48, 50, 51, 59, 74, 82, 83, 85, 87

L

Laodice, 33, 34
Little Horn, 21
Lysimachus, 31, 32

M

Martin Luther, 67, 68, 69
Medo-Persia, 17
Moab, 83, 84, 85

Muslim, 74, 82, 83, 91, 93, 102

O

Ottoman Empire, 74

P

Palestine, 31, 83
Papacy, 64, 66, 67, 69, 70, 71, 77, 81, 89, 90, 91, 93, 94, 101
Papal supremacy, 65, 69, 74
Persia, 26, 27, 30, 40, 88
Pompey Magnus, 43
Pope, 56, 57, 70
Pope Pius VI, 71
Prince of the Covenant, 47
Protestant Reformation, 68
Ptolemy I Soter, 31
Ptolemy II, 33, 34
Ptolemy III, 34, 35
Ptolemy IV, 36, 37
Ptolemy V, 37, 38, 42
Ptolemy VI, 39
Ptolemy XIV, 43

R

Rome, 16, 40, 42, 44, 47, 48, 49, 50, 51, 52, 53, 55, 56, 57, 58,

S

Sabbath, 5, 64, 66, 99
Seleucus I Nicator, 31, 32
Seleucus II, 34, 35

T

Temporal millennium, 93, 96, 97
The Battle of Panium, 37
The Battle of Raphia, 36
The Beast, 80
The God of forces, 75, 76
The Ottoman Empire, 74
The Third Syrian War, 33
The War of the Brothers, 35
Tiberius Caesar, 46

U

United States, 4, 80, 81, 82, 83, 85, 86, 88, 90, 91

V

Vandalic War, 57, 58
Vandalism, 50
Vandals, 48, 49, 50, 51, 52, 57, 58

www.ingramcontent.com/pod-product-compliance
Lightning Source LLC
Chambersburg PA
CBHW062022290426
44108CB00024B/2748